EVOLUTIONARY RELIGION

Evolutionary Religion

J. L. SCHELLENBERG

OXFORD
UNIVERSITY PRESS

OXFORD
UNIVERSITY PRESS

Great Clarendon Street, Oxford, OX2 6DP,
United Kingdom

Oxford University Press is a department of the University of Oxford.
It furthers the University's objective of excellence in research, scholarship,
and education by publishing worldwide. Oxford is a registered trade mark of
Oxford University press in the UK and in certain other countries

© J. L. Schellenberg 2013

The moral rights of the author have been asserted

First Edition published in 2013

Impression: 1

British Library Cataloguing in Publication Data

Data available

Library of Congress Cataloging in Publication Data

Data available

ISBN 978-0-19-967376-6

Printed in Great Britain by
MPG Books Group, Bodmin and King's Lynn

For Regina

Note to the Reader

If you ever feel, while reading, that something needs a deeper treatment, it could be that it receives such treatment—at the end of the book. There, among the notes, you will find occasional comments that take a bit further what is being discussed in the text. They were left out of the text to avoid disrupting the flow.

Contents

Acknowledgments

Most of the people who helped me with this book are dead. I have in mind Charles Darwin, John Stuart Mill, William James, and ever so many others. Fortunately this fact is compatible with there being very many who have helped me among the living. I want to tender my thanks to them all.

First on the list is my wife, the artist Regina Coupar. She came last last time. So now she knows she is, for me, both first and last. She also comes first in the book since it is dedicated to her. Regina bought me a couple of great works on Darwin at a time when I was just starting to make some vital evolutionary connections. After hearing and responding to multiple versions of my ideas from a bracingly unconventional perspective, she was still willing to read the final final draft and give me many additional useful thoughts. A member of my family who got to know her back in the late nineties, shortly after she came into my life, said to me: "You are a very fortunate man." That was—and is—the truth.

My cousin, Maggie Redekop, Professor Emerita in the Department of English at the University of Toronto, read the prior-to-penultimate draft and sent me a great many very helpful comments which I appreciated all the more since they afforded me the perspective of someone quite happily *not* a philosopher! I am very grateful to her for doing so, and also for stimulating follow-up conversations.

Much discussion in a variety of settings with my good friends Paul Draper and Dan Howard-Snyder has, I think, brought our views in the philosophy of religion closer together. In any case, I'm grateful to both for always being willing to help me think things through. To Dan I owe special thanks for his extensive and very useful comments on the penultimate version of the book, at a time when he was up to his ears in work—some of it already helpful to me in other ways.

I've also learned much, while preparing this book, from several symposia on my recent trilogy held at meetings of the Canadian Philosophical Association in Montreal and at meetings of the American Philosophical Association in Minneapolis and Seattle. Jason Marsh and John Thorp organized the former and Dan Howard-Snyder the latter. I am very grateful to them, to the audience members, and of course to all the commentators, who (in addition to Dan and Jason) included: Paul Draper, Jack MacIntosh, Steve Wykstra, Terence Cuneo, Andrew Chignell, Wes Morriston, Andrew Dole, Jeanine Diller, Tom Crisp, and Terry Penelhum.

Looking back over the last few years, thinking about who else has—perhaps without knowing it—helped me try to write this very different sort of book, I remember Richard Swinburne, Ingolf Dalferth, Steve Maitzen, Don Wiebe, Ivan Khan, Yiftach Fehige, John Cottingham, Robert Audi, and Bob Adams. My thanks to each of them.

Finally, let me express my gratitude to all of the talented and very professional people at Oxford University Press who helped put this book together, including especially Peter Momtchiloff. The comments of an anonymous reviewer for Oxford University Press are also much appreciated.

My sincerest gratitude to everyone. To anyone whom I may have left out inadvertently: you have both my gratitude and my apologies.

Prologue: Deep Time Religion

I'm an analytical philosopher. Readers don't always react with enthusiasm to such a confession, and recently I was told why. Apparently there's a commodity considered valuable in literature called "narrative tension," a.k.a. suspense. But analytical philosophers, given their penchant for directness and precision, don't have much use for suspense. A detective novel written by a good philosopher would begin: "In this novel I shall show that the butler did it."

I thought it interesting that it was a philosopher who told the joke. Forgotten is what remedy, if any, he prescribed for philosophers addressing a wider audience, one including non-philosophers. But we may not need a remedy here. For what I intend to show is not unrelated to story and suspense. You've already noticed that the book is about evolution and religion. One way of introducing my take on this subject is to say that the story of evolution and religion, as most of us have heard it, is at best a story *half told* which we have been treating as the whole story. I want us to get started on the rest of the story.

So sit back, relax . . . and expect to be drawn to the edge of your seat in suspense!

* * *

At least since Darwin, religion and evolution have tended to be at odds. Often they have resembled nothing so much as schoolchildren glaring at each other across the room, shoving or tripping one another in the hall. Although evolutionists have had great hopes of stimulating positive developments in fields as various as medicine and education, in matters religious even the most optimistic and conciliatory among them hope for little more than that evolution and religion may learn to sit side by side quietly without kicking each other under the table.

No doubt the very public and acrimonious debates we've seen over biological evolution are part of the reason for this adversarial relationship. According to the Darwinian theory of evolution through natural selection, those organisms best adjusted to their environment survive and pass on their traits, and over truly enormous periods of time this natural process leads to a complex accumulation of adaptive changes in their populations mimicking intelligent design. Naturally enough, this result has been taken by many as competing with the idea of real Divine design.

But these battles over biology are deeply intertwined with a broader struggle over how we should design *ourselves*. Enter another—though related—form of evolution called "cultural evolution" (the term refers to changes in our species over time generated by cultural factors.) Though cultural evolution, like biological, concerns what does happen, it is often because of what someone thinks *should* happen—going to the moon, giving women the vote, putting an end to war—that it occurs. And there are plenty of writers who quite apart from Darwinian loyalties on matters biological would like to see religion trimmed from human culture, delighting in the exposure of everything antiquated or bloated or grotesque that lurks in its shadows. They think of religion as an aberration in the human experiment, unworthy of "humanity come of age." Not surprisingly, science they regard as representing the way forward. The well known author and journalist Christopher Hitchens speaks for such an orientation when, in his book *God is not Great*, he writes that religion belongs to "the infancy of our species."

On some days, it's not hard to sympathize with this point of view. Much ignobility has been sponsored by unthinking religious conviction. But seeking a wider vantage point, and aiming only for understanding, what we will find, I suggest, is a mistake built on an oversight. The mistake is the supposition that cultural evolution of a sort we should approve, gaining speed with the discovery of natural evolution, must roll over religion rather than redeeming it—must savage it rather than saving it. And the oversight, which I shall be combating at some length in this book, is ironically our collective failure to take note of our place in time as the evolutionary sciences understand it and to recognize that the elevated point to which evolution has brought us on our planet still marks no more than the very beginning of intelligent life. (I put readers on notice that I will be taking "intelligence" very broadly in this book, including within the range of the term anything properly called emotional intelligence as well as any similarly sensitive capacity.)

Evolutionary time is of an extent almost beyond fathoming—that's why scientists call it "deep." The Harvard biologist and paleontologist, Stephen Jay Gould, put it this way: "an abstract, intellectual understanding of deep time comes easily enough—I know how many zeroes to place after the 10 when I mean billions. Getting it into the gut is another matter." Because of the efforts of scientists like Gould, we've been starting to internalize Darwin's idea of natural selection occurring over many millions of years. But the truly enormous periods of time required for something like *Homo sapiens* to be evolutionarily produced still give many members of that limited species a stomach ache.

And that's just the deep past. What about the deep future? Here we've been especially slow to get all the relevant zeroes into the gut—so slow as to have hardly begun the digestion process. It is especially this slowness, as we'll see, that allows for certain unnoticed chapters in the story of evolution and religion. Here's another way of putting the point: we've so far experienced no more than "half a revolution" in our thinking about time—the revolution involving our discovery and slow comprehension of the deep past. To deal adequately with certain subjects including religion we need to be able to do better. We need to be able to convert our mental clocks easily to scientific time both past and future. But this aspect of scientific literacy is not yet widely discernible among us.

To acquire it, one needs to think hard about the fact that the perhaps 200,000-year history of *H. sapiens* is wedged between three and a half billion years of evolutionary development on one side—life's past—and another billion on the other—life's potential future. Consider especially the second figure. A billion years is a period of time ridiculously longer than the 50,000 years of thinking and feeling that, on a generous estimate, our species has put into religion so far. What *developments* in religiously-relevant thought and feeling might Earth see in so much time?

Even if we restrict ourselves to the possible future of our own species, the numbers are staggering. *H. sapiens*, though manifesting its religious inclinations and symbolic powers a bit earlier, has at most 6,000 years of organized and systematic religious inquiry to its credit. This is also the age of the longest-lived of those traditions we regard as the venerable Great World Religions. The average lifespan of hominid or—following an emerging terminological preference in science—*hominin* species (the 20 or so known species on our branch of the evolutionary tree) is roughly 800,000 years. So we might realistically hope that members of *H. sapiens* will endure and continue putting their big brains to work for at least another 600,000 years. And 6,000 years between 200,000 on one side and 600,000 on the other surely counts as a very modest beginning! Suppose we take an individual human life of eighty years to represent the 800,000 years our species may last. We would then have to be regarded as being something like a twenty-year-old who only started thinking about religion some six months ago. Of course someone is bound to observe that our species may not make it past twenty-one. But this doesn't prevent its experience with religion so far from being properly regarded, in scientific terms, as extremely brief, or its immaturity from grounding a rather far-reaching religious skepticism.

As these thoughts suggest, my own analysis of the relationship between evolution and religion, like that of Hitchens, refers to the infancy of the species, but I believe I see things rather differently than he does. Hitchens seems to have in mind the distant past—*that's* where religion should have stayed—whereas in my sense of the word, which is science's, we are still very much *living through* the infancy of our species. "In the beginning" begins the biblical book of Genesis. But anyone who really makes the shift from human to scientific timescales will see that we are still in the beginning. We've never left it. The beginning is now. And precisely in this scientific idea of our infancy, I want to suggest, there lies hidden a means of altogether transforming our usual picture of evolution and religion as adversaries.

I don't mean only—as might be expected—that however sharp one's critique of current religious beliefs, one can't rule out the possibility of profound religious insights in the future. This is part of what I want to emphasize but decidedly not the whole. No, the consequences of the deep future for religion are far more interesting than that, exposing also a new way of thinking about religion in the present. The key is to notice an intriguing question about evolution and religion that has not yet been raised in the religion debates: *Is there a form of religion appropriate to our place in evolutionary time?* More precisely: Is there a religious way of life that is made admirable or desirable by the features of *our* moment in evolutionary time as distinct from others? The idea here is that if indeed we are at the beginning of intelligent doings on our planet instead of at the end, then we ought to consider whether there are any religious behaviors—perhaps ones somewhat different from those to which we've grown accustomed—that might *fit* such a beginning.

Only from an evolutionary stance involving careful reflection on deep time, with the latter conception taken from where it now sits tightly bunched at the junction of past and present and unrolled into the far future—only from here can this question even be seen. And my point is that only when it *is* seen can we start to think about religion in fully evolutionary terms. Although what will emerge when we do is initially a new form of forward-looking evolutionary skepticism or doubt applicable both to religious and to irreligious beliefs (which must now appear premature, quite *in*appropriate to our place in time), close on its heels will come a new answer to the cultural difficulties religion faces and, with it, the possibility of a new form of religion deeply rooted in evolutionary thought.

The book is divided into four pairs of chapters. The first pair offers more on the science of deep time, and the second pair draws out its skeptical consequences. (Chapter 3 is perhaps the most difficult in the book and I won't mind if, after sampling it, you skip over to Chapter 4 with its religious application of skeptical ideas.) The third pair of chapters—which begins the second half of the book—explains how this science and skepticism have the surprising effect just mentioned of opening up new space for religious thinking, and how the possibility of a new form of religion or religiousness, properly called *evolutionary religion*, is suggested. The last pair of chapters defends my view on this positive and liberating turn of events against some basic objections and also shows how one might reason in support of the idea that the new religiousness I have outlined is indeed appropriate to our place in time. Because I have been much inspired by the life and work of Charles Darwin during the time of writing, he will be appearing, in one role or another, in most of my chapters.

As this summary makes clear, I will in the book be offering my own candidate for the status of "a form of religion deeply rooted in evolutionary thought" and my own answer to the unstudied question raised above: a form of religion living on imagination rather than belief that could be right for us and open the door to positive cultural evolution even if other forms of religion are wrong. My candidate idea aims to be both grand in conception and morally attractive while retaining better prospects for long-term survival among inquiring minds than most of what's on our minds today.

But I want to emphasize that my interest is much less in publicizing a new form of religion than in getting us to think seriously about the idea of evolutionary religion in the first place and note its potential importance—considering how evolution and religion can be deeply harmonized by asking what sort of faith might be appropriate to our place in time. Some philosophers have interpreted the ideas I'll be outlining in the final chapters of the book as presupposing the aim to start a new religious movement, perhaps one more able to satisfy my existential needs than others I have loved and left in the past! But this is a misinterpretation. The term "evolutionary religion" refers not to some specific religious form of life that I am looking to defend and for which I am seeking converts but rather to an *object of inquiry* or a possible type of thing: a form of religion we all might assess positively given a fuller evolutionary picture, and, in particular, one that is admirable or desirable given the specific features of the place we occupy in time—a very early one. Could there be such a thing? What might it look like? Might investigation of the first two questions lead to an interesting new way of dealing with problems of religion in modern culture? These are the matters that most deeply provoke my interest. Of course I presently hold that the answer to each question is Yes and intend to explain why. But my main aim is to get us thinking about such questions. We have not thought about religion in a temporalist way before—"temporalism" is my name for the position that emphasizes our place in time and the importance of bending our thought accordingly—and I believe much may be illuminated if we do. It is this that excites me. But I do not pretend to bring all of this illumination in the present volume. And my ideas about skeptical-imaginative religion are intended as a first word not the last.

I have developed similar views before in three books, a trilogy, aimed at philosophers and written over the past decade. But not until recently did I see clearly the evolutionary framework that was, as it were, waiting to receive all my results. In this book I seek to hammer it out and make my case anew, putting it forward as a proposal to the wider intellectual community and indeed to all who are interested in whether religion can or ought to survive. The ongoing debates over science and religion tend to presuppose that it is *old* time religion that must appear in our future, if any does. By thinking in the right ways about *deep* time possibilities of faith, I hope we will come to recognize this idea for the ungrounded prejudice in favor of a familiar past that it really is, and to see the idea of evolutionary religion as one whose time has come.

1

Half a Revolution

> Our brains are built to deal with events on radically different
> *timescales* from those that characterize evolutionary change. We
> are equipped to appreciate processes that take seconds, minutes,
> years or, at most, decades to complete. Darwinism is a theory of
> processes so slow that they take between thousands and millions
> of decades to complete. . . . It requires effort of the imagination
> to escape from the prison of familiar timescale.
>
> Richard Dawkins, *The Blind Watchmaker*

I live on the South Shore of Nova Scotia in a big old house overlook-
ing the ocean. It was built by a local sea captain in 1883—just a year
after Charles Darwin died. In the woods back of the house where
I walk nearly every day are scattered many large granite boulders
known as glacial erratics. They are the farewell gifts of an ice sheet
that was slowly departing the region, gouging lakes as it went, about
10,000 years before my house went up. Walking by a particularly
impressive chunk of granite tall as myself, trailing a hand across its
rough crystalline surface, I often marvel over how incredibly long it
has lain (more or less) right there!

This information and such experiences are mine courtesy of the
decidedly unflashy but revolutionary science of geology, to which the
flashier sciences traceable to Darwin owe a great deal. And geology
tells me more. It tells me that 10,000 years is as nothing compared to
the long ages that have passed since my favorite rock was first formed
through the cooling of magma at a time of intense plate tectonic
activity some 400 million years ago. (Its crystals bear mute testimony
to this event.) It tells me, too, that these are only moments in a much
larger story stretching back billions of years. In that time, continents
have traveled the globe, crunched into each other, and fallen apart.

Oceans have come and gone. Climates have waxed and waned. Of course even if you had had a ringside seat throughout the eons of time that have passed, and been able to watch it all, you would never really have achieved the sense that you saw it happen: things in nature take place far too slowly for that. But over vast periods of time, the simplest forms of life have slowly evolved into multi-celled plants and animals including human beings, whose tread on the landscape is leaving the deepest marks of all.

I'm pretty sure that the indigenous Mi'kmaq, the Acadians who had a few settlements in this area in the seventeenth century, the German Lutherans who founded nearby Lunenburg in 1753, and also the sea captain who built my house had somewhat different ideas. They won't have seen the ocean or surrounding hills or their plants and animals or themselves or my rock back in the woods quite as I do. And, certainly for the non-natives in the group, "a very long time ago" would take the imagination back only about as far as the time of Jesus or Moses—which is to say, only a few thousand years. It's in part because of the profound tendency of sciences such as geology and biology, and also physics and astronomy, to expand our sense of time, awakening new thoughts about our place in nature, that these sciences are rightly called revolutionary.

THE DISCOVERY OF DEEP TIME

But it has proved very difficult for humans to get their heads around the stupendous vastness of the past. Deep time is time of a very different order. Its ways are not our ways. As the British ethologist and evolutionary biologist Richard Dawkins has aptly said: "Our brains are built to deal with events on radically different *timescales* from those that characterize evolutionary change. . . . It requires effort of the imagination to escape from the prison of familiar timescale."

Indeed. Recognizing this limitation in ourselves, maybe it's not too hard to see why it took a while for deep time to be discovered by human beings. It didn't aid discovery that the systematic exploration of nature, using methods broadly resembling ones familiar today, began only during the scientific revolution of the sixteenth and seventeenth centuries. True, long before the sixteenth century far-sighted and observant thinkers like Aristotle were guessing that the

Earth is much older than generally thought. But to displace seemingly intuitive ideas, especially ones that have had a long time to settle, striking evidence is necessary. And this was just not available until thinkers really got into the business of looking for nature's laws in the careful and collaborative manner, guided by detailed experimentation and field research, that is the hallmark of science.

A famous early episode of geological field research features one of the most striking pieces of evidence for deep time that was ever unearthed and also a nice example of how our primitive faculties are affected by such things. This occurred one summer's day in 1788, when the great British geologist James Hutton showed his friend John Playfair an "unconformity" at Siccar Point in Scotland.

An unconformity is an ancient erosion surface dividing two layers of rock which, in shape, do not "conform" to one another. What Playfair saw were vertically tilted rocks on the bottom and horizontal ones on top. And what he was invited to consider was that this pairing is incompatible with the traditional picture of a young Earth gradually surrendering its earthiness in an uninterrupted process of erosion to the sea. Instead, what the bottom layer showed was that the ocean had been the scene of rock being pushed back *up* when the compacted sediment from erosion on land, deposited in horizontal layers on the ocean floor, produced sufficient pressure and heat to generate a hugely forceful uplift. And it showed that rock broke and tilted steeply upward as new land was formed above the ocean's surface. The new land was then itself eroded by the same forces that caused the former erosion, resulting in the unconformity surface, which eventually found itself under water serving as a basis on which fresh sedimentary layers could horizontally be deposited. When uplift again occurred, as it had to, for the same physical reasons as before, rock once again rose above the surface but this time without becoming deformed through breaking and tilting—resulting in the "horizontal above vertical" rock formations that Playfair saw.

Hutton told his friend that the Earth was a machine, repeatedly running through a cycle with stages of erosion, deposition, compacting, and uplift. Any one cycle took unbelievably long to unfold, and given that each led naturally to another, the repeated cycling might always have been going on.

"Pretty neat!" said Playfair. Well, not quite. What he actually wrote when recording the event later that day is this: "The impression made will not easily be forgotten." And then he added: "The mind seemed to grow giddy by looking so far into the abyss of time."

Later Hutton was able to confirm that many rocks on the Earth's surface were—like my crystal-studded granite in the woods—igneous, not sedimentary, formed when magma from deep below intruded, cooled, and was solidified. This provided further evidence for his theory of an eroded world continually and mechanically restored, with one continent following another virtually endlessly. His theory of the Earth as a continent-breaking-and-making-machine, at least when rescued from his own somewhat obscure prose by Playfair's beautifully written restatement, *Illustrations of the Huttonian Theory of the Earth*, marked the beginning of an important breakthrough in our understanding of the Earth's past.

Hutton's work gave geology, and with it a startling new picture of time, its first big boost. But many others were to follow. The "uniformitarianism" (as it came to be called) that animates Hutton's work—the idea that the Earth has been shaped over immense periods by processes still at work today—was greatly developed and extended by Sir Charles Lyell in his *Principles of Geology*, written when both he and the nineteenth century were in their thirties. The multi-volume book would be successively refined by him until, with the twelfth revision around him, the great man died in his (and the century's) seventies.

Lyell and other geologists of that century did their own pioneering, too. They were able to work out how the layering of rocks—stratification—and also the very diverse fossils different strata contained could help science discern the various periods of change and development the Earth had undergone, as well as how long they had lasted. Indeed, a multitude of divisions had to be made, which is why geology at last came to speak not only of periods but—and here I favor the North American side of a terminological continental divide—of supereons, eons, eras, periods, epochs, and ages.

At first the dating of various intervals was very approximate, guided by such crude measures as observed rates of weathering in rocks. It generated much controversy. In the late nineteenth century, controversy intensified when physics got in on the act. The great physicist William Thomson, later to become Lord Kelvin, thought the Earth was cooling from an originally molten state; its heat was greater than the Sun alone could generate. Using his discoveries in thermodynamics and employing early models of solar evolution, which knew nothing of nuclear energy, Thomson was led to constantly shrinking estimates of the Earth's age (24 million years, in his last pronouncement). Thus when Charles Darwin died in 1882, it was still quite unclear whether the enormously long and meandering processes of natural selection his theory of evolution predicted could be stuffed into the temporal space available. Darwin's writings show that he experienced considerable anxiety over the issue.

But everything changed with the discovery, a quarter century later, of radioactivity and nuclear energy. This provided an explanation for heat from within the Earth itself and—not incidentally—allowed for a much longer-lived Sun. On the heels of these discoveries came the enormous advance of radiometric dating, pioneered by the chemist-physicist Ernest Rutherford and developed by the geologist Arthur Holmes in the early decades of the twentieth century, who learned to read what—in a manner suggesting that somewhere there is a geological Dr Seuss—are called "clocks in rocks": radioactive elements that break down at a measurable rate. Once content to think in terms of millions of years (already a huge step beyond the 6,000 years or so of popular belief), scientists were now comfortably speaking of the Earth as perhaps two or three billion years old. With further tests and refinements and applications of radiometric dating in the twentieth century, those time spans were stretched still further. Rocks more than four billion years old would eventually be found on the Earth's surface, and based on the tight web of information from the various sciences bearing on deep time, the age of the Earth is today pegged at about 4.54 billion years.

Lord Kelvin would be surprised—and Charles Darwin relieved!

THE OTHER SIDE OF TIME

All this is a fairly conventional retelling of one chapter in the history of science. Such a retelling suffices to show that we are starting to get used to the fact of deep time. But precisely because the story is conventional, covering all the bases usually covered, it is hard to avoid noticing that deep time is still somewhat onesidedly associated with the deep *past*. The imaginative devices employed to help us get a feel for deep time inevitably start from the beginning of Earth's history and end with our rather recent arrival on the scene. If that history were compressed into the hour between 11 p.m. and midnight, we are breathlessly told, humans would appear just a fraction of a second before midnight! Or, as John McPhee has famously put it: "If the history of the Earth were represented by the old English measure of a yard, the distance from the king's nose to the end of his outstretched hand, all of human history could be erased by a single stroke of a file on his middle fingernail."

Okay. That's impressive. And hard enough on the imagination. But to see our place in time—to achieve what I will be calling "temporal contextualization"—we need to tell the *whole* story, including the bits about the other side of time. We need to remember the deep future.

The long future of our planet, and in particular its long period of further habitability, is every bit as scientifically-credentialed as its long past. Here the Sun is central to the story. Science has learned a great deal this century about stars like our Sun, developing a general theory of their origin and evolution through observation of many different star clusters of different ages, and by studying the physics of individual stars of different masses. In a lecture at the Perkins Observatory in 1997, Richard Pogge, Professor of Astronomy at Ohio State University, put it this way: "An understanding of the process of stellar evolution is one of the great triumphs of twentieth century astrophysics. . . . We are now sufficiently confident of our results that an apparent discrepancy between the ages of the oldest stars in the Galaxy and the estimated age of the Universe is thought by many to signal weaknesses in our understanding of the evolution of the Universe rather than problems with the theory of stellar evolution."

So what can be derived from these brave new explorations of the sky about the future of life here on Earth? Well, the Sun has been getting steadily brighter and hotter since it first was formed; the standard model of solar evolution, developed in the 1980s by Douglas Gough, now Professor of Astronomy at Cambridge, puts its original luminosity at about 70 percent of its current value. Consequently, at a certain point the average temperature on Earth will reach heights incompatible with the persistence of life on its surface. The biosphere, no longer able to adjust, will succumb.

But at what point? When conditions on the planet no longer allow for the presence of liquid water, is the usual answer. This answer is also given by astrophysicists K. P. Schroeder of the Universidad de Guanajuato and Robert Connon Smith of the University of Sussex in their widely cited paper "Distant future of the sun and earth revisited," published in the *Monthly Notices of the Royal Astronomical Society* in 2008. And when do they think our oceans will be sucked dry? Their model predicts it will be when the Sun's luminosity has been increased by another 10 percent. By their calculations, "the present Sun is increasing its average luminosity at a rate of 1 percent in every 110 million years," which will amount to about "10 percent over the next billion years." Accordingly, Schroeder and Smith conclude that our planet will lose its cosmic AAA rating of "habitable" in a billion years.

Their study only confirms what has for some time been thought, and what has been inscribed in many an astronomy textbook. Thus it confirms Pogge's point about the considerable stability of astrophysics over recent decades. Schroeder and Smith are themselves quick to point out the consistency of their results with established models. Now, present science may of course be superseded in certain respects. But the implications of any scientific evolution for the prediction of a billion year future are as likely to be intensifying as undermining. (The authors of this paper observe in passing that realistic means of nudging Earth's orbit outward to delay overheating are already being contemplated by scientists.) So we have to take the point seriously.

In fact, shortly after I wrote that paragraph, I came across another paper, written a year later by a team of scientists at Caltech, that does intensify—or more correctly, that radically enlarges—the previously accepted figure of a billion years. Interestingly, it does so without contesting basic results in astrophysics. As its title suggests, the paper "Atmospheric pressure as a natural climate regulator for a terrestrial planet with a biosphere," published in the *Proceedings of the National Academy of Sciences* in 2009, looks to factors nearer home to provide the extension. And what an extension! *Time* magazine on June 15, 2009 proclaimed it with a big 2.3 in the "numbers" section of its briefing page: 2.3 billion years, more than twice the official figure.

What generated the new figure? Answer: the hypothesized natural fluctuation of atmospheric pressure over really, really long periods of time. As the Caltech press release explained, if atmospheric pressure has diminished once in a while throughout Earth's history, then the "holes" in the blanket of greenhouse gases will from time to time have been enlarged, allowing the planet to absorb less heat and thus postponing the biosphere's inevitable demise. This trick of nature hadn't previously been considered because, in the absence of evidence to the contrary, science has always assumed that atmospheric pressure doesn't vary over time. But King-Fai Li and the other Caltech scientists think it has varied, and indeed that it is now lower than it was in the past, because of natural mechanisms removing from the atmosphere one of its major gases: nitrogen. Procedures have already been devised to test for this, and the tests are being undertaken. So we should soon be able to tell whether the hypothesis of the Caltech team is confirmed and the excitement of people at *Time* warranted.

But soon isn't now. Because such confirmation has not yet been achieved, I will, in the present discussion, stick with the round figure of a billion years. This figure is quite safe, and it is certainly large enough. Indeed, it could be halved many times over and still provide all the support needed for the argument to come. These temporal differences, involving millions of years, may of course seem rather more significant than that. But this is because, even when we do consider periods of time lasting that long, we fall into treating them like much shorter periods. We worry at the thought that the Earth will be scorched by the Sun in a billion years, and rejoice at a billion-year extension. This only shows that we haven't yet grasped what "billion" really means here! Recalling Gould, we haven't quite got it "into the gut."

So how can we do better? How can we begin to imagine a future for life that long and picture how it relates to paths already taken, including paths taken in systematic inquiry—thus helping along the second half of a revolution in thought? Recycling imaginative devices deployed for the past, we could, I suppose, think about compressing the possibly billion-year-long future of life on Earth into the hour *after* midnight, noting that the period of our systematically reflective activities so far would take us only a couple of seconds or so into that hour. But other imaginative devices are also available.

One, which I used earlier today with my ethics students, involves a twenty-foot chalk line. My students were wondering why, after all the time that philosophers have spent discussing theoretical questions concerning right and wrong, good and bad, we should still lack consensus on the answers. So I drew a line from one end of my long blackboard to the other (yes, I'm one of those unreconstructed teachers who likes to walk and talk with chalk), a distance of twenty feet. That distance, I told them, represents a period of about a billion years, extending from the time when our brain cells first really started clicking some 50,000 years ago until the time in the future when the

Sun's slowly encroaching heat will make Earth uninhabitable by all life, whether intelligent or not. Forbidding the clicking of calculators, I then asked my students for their impressions as to how much of that line intelligence had already occupied. What portion of it had been traversed?

The answers they ventured were invariably too generous, wildly inaccurate. That's because even bringing the estimate back to a single small inch still leaves one incredibly far from the truth. To get it close to right, I informed them, you'd have to think of the distance already covered as a mere one eighty-third of an inch—a distance invisible to the naked eye. And if instead of generously going back 50,000 years we start the line at 6,000 years before the present, which is roughly when human civilization arose, that distance is diminished to about one seven-hundredth of an inch. If—even more realistically in my classroom—we start from 2,500 years ago, when systematic philosophizing in the west began, the relevant distance is vanishingly small: a single one-thousand-six hundred-and-eightieth of an inch.

So cut an inch into one thousand six hundred and eighty pieces and the first of those bits represents how far philosophical inquiry has traveled through time so far, with virtually all of twenty feet (403,199 more such bits, to be exact) representing the temporal distance remaining! My point, of course, was that it's still early days in philosophy. Using a scientific lens, we have to say that intelligence is only now coming into being on our planet.

A second device we can use to help us imagine how far we've traveled, and how much further there may be to go, involves all the words in this book. It requires that you *forget* the words and try to think only of the letters composing them. Think of each of those letters as representing a century. Now slowly turn (or imagine yourself turning) each page of the book, drawing your finger down the page, deliberately thinking of what you see on each page not as words but as a collection of letters and thinking of each letter on all those pages as a century. Only a handful of lines on the first page is needed to net you the five hundred centuries reflective intelligence on our planet has had so far. But even when you get to the end of the whole book, you will still have a representation of only about one-tenth of the total number of centuries Earthly intelligence *may* have. (And this is without taking into account the time that intelligence from Earth may win for itself by planting its intelligence elsewhere.) You'd need to flip through at least another nine books of equal length to take note of the number of letters representing the number of centuries that may see intelligence on our planet.

After pausing to let that sink in, take things one step further. As you pass your mental gaze over all of the letters coming after the first few lines in that pile of books, strewn across thousands of pages, imagining each one as a century, imagine also that by touching any letter you could pull up a list of changes in the circumstances affecting intelligent life as great as have, on average, attended the past five hundred centuries. (That limit is fairly generous to the cynic, since until recently, development has often been very slow: large chunks of human history have gone by with very little to alter the fundamental features of human existence.) And mentally add and subtract imaginary accomplishments as you take in all the millions of centuries to come, applying everything you know about science and human ingenuity, chance and design, sifting, allowing for the fits and starts of evolution. What might we have by the end?

We might, of course, have nothing at all. This is a possibility brought home to us by familiar doomsday scenarios involving such things as the impact of an enormous asteroid or the eruption of megavolcanoes. Some worry that in one nasty way or another intelligence on Earth will be wiped from its face within the *next* century, so that thinking of the next ten million or even ten is, to say the least, fanciful. But for every such bad possibility facing us today, there's a myriad of bad-canceling ones whose likelihoods are hard to assess but must be known if we are to establish how likely that bad possibility is. Perhaps this explains why in his book, *Our Final Century*, the former Astronomer Royal, Sir Martin Rees, cautiously—and somewhat belying his grim title—puts the odds that we will survive the twenty-first century at "fifty-fifty."

Now, that is a worrisome figure, and I by no means wish to suggest otherwise. The task facing human beings in the immediate future is indeed urgent, and it would be as exasperatingly irresponsible to replace our chronic short-term thinking with excessively or onesidedly long-term thinking as not to replace it at all. But while I strongly commend Rees' work and aims, my purpose here is somewhat different from the purpose that animates such books (though as you'll see when we come to consider what religion should be about, it is ultimately consilient with them). My purpose requires us to stand back, for a moment, from matters of strictly human concern.

Setting on one side, then, our natural human self-preoccupation, let's think a bit more carefully about what it would take to really be left with "nothing at all" in the way of intelligent life at the end of the next billion years. Life on Earth is nothing if not tenacious. If disasters occur but intelligent life and its possible precursors are not completely extinguished, a billion years provides a lot of time for recovery and improvement. We need to remember that it took only about five million years to get from the apes to us. A billion years affords two hundred times that amount of time for something similar or even more dramatically interesting to occur.

With doomsday scenarios put in their place, as representing one easy-to-exaggerate possibility among others, a surge of new questions must be experienced. What enormous changes might be effected in ten million centuries, by processes much slower than we can readily notice (or swifter than we expect, if genetic manipulation or artificial intellectual enhancements enter the mix), as forms of life continue to adapt to their environments? Might we lose much more of our propensity to violence? Might it be only if we are able to survive far into the future that we will develop fitness for understanding the really sensitive and subtle and profound things? Might the totality of human thought be some small part in a long story involving other species that has hardly begun to be written—a few paragraphs back on page 2 or 1? And how much of those paragraphs does our present thinking represent? Would it be so much as a full sentence? What words, ultimately, will be spoken?

The ludicrous difference or, as I like to call it, the *Great Disparity* between how far intelligence has come on our planet and how much further it may yet have to go should stop us in our tracks. Properly absorbed, it is hugely impressive. But we almost never think about such things. How often, for example, do we think in detail about the glaciation cycles to come, or the possible return of our individual continents to a supercontinent, or *any* of the myriad of live possibilities involving new and interesting forms of life that may be realized on our planet as what we call the twenty-first century is succeeded by the twenty-second and the twenty-third and the twenty-fourth and not just tens or hundreds but thousands and millions of centuries more? One wonders why evolutionary thinkers like Dawkins don't prod us more about such facts—why they don't think much more about the changes we might hope to see in another million centuries, given all that has occurred in just the last five hundred, or twenty, or one. Perhaps it would be helpful if we summoned *here* the "effort of the imagination to escape from the prison of familiar timescale" that Dawkins rightly recommends.

TIME OUT OF MIND

So why haven't humans yet done so? Well, we certainly shouldn't forget simple human self-preoccupation. The line of evolution reaches us, and we find it hard to imagine it moving further. Mightily impressed with ourselves, we give little thought to the idea of beings who may come after us.

But we also have to contend with neural programming that makes it hard to do better: the slowly-evolving human brain still spends a lot of time worrying about what amounted to immediate challenges during the Pleistocene Age. As the *New York Times* columnist Nicholas Kristof, reporting on neurological studies, recently put it: "If you come across a garter snake, nearly all of your brain will light up with activity as you process the 'threat.' Yet if somebody tells you that carbon emissions will eventually destroy Earth as we know it, only the small part of the brain that focuses on the future—a portion of the prefrontal cortex—will glimmer." Evolution itself may bear part of the responsibility for our neglect of evolution's future.

Such facts may help to explain why the scientific timescale involving billions of years of Earthly change is just formidably difficult for a species like ours to internalize. It is a point that sadly affects all of us—scientists and philosophers included—and it explains a lot. But now add this further point, about what we may call the "psychological priority of the past." Where we've been exerting the requisite imagination, it has, as we've seen, tended to take us *back* in time.

Plausible reasons for this one-sidedness in our temporal imagination are not hard to find. There is no bed of deposits where one can dig up fossils providing us with evidence as to future events. So what is there to hold our attention? And of course it is by discovering the deep past that we discovered deep time in the first place. Moreover, the view looking back is certainly captivating and preoccupying, as dozens of Discovery Channel specials attest. Things that happened there, in the recesses of evolutionary time, touch us deeply, affecting our very sense of identity.

Furthermore, it should be borne in mind, as we consider these matters, that we haven't been taking in that view for very long: the discovery of deep past time is actually quite a recent event. Remember that it was only in 1788 that the encounter between Hutton and Playfair took place. More time may be needed for us really to absorb deep time and its ramifications. Here we need also to remember that many things central to the shaping of western culture, such as the formation of the Bible, come well before the discovery of deep time. Naturally enough, given the human timescales by which we live, Bible-based thinking about events has tended to assume a rather *short* Earthly history—thousands of years instead of millions or billions. Such thinking has therefore been in an excellent position to exert a serious "drag effect" on our consciousness of time's true extent. The deep past, indeed, has proven quite difficult to get into the gut. As the continuing debate over the teaching of evolution attests, many are still choking on it.

These things conspire to make it the case that all of us are, in a way, stuck in the past. But of course without noticing the deep future, we can't picture the Great Disparity. And without seeing the Great Disparity, we will have a skewed picture of deep time and what it really means for us.

Consider only how different things look in the two ways presented in Figure 1 (below) of contextualizing, temporally, the short 50,000-year period of characteristically human intellectual activity (which, with a bow in the direction of our self-centeredness, I have denominated US).

In the top part of Figure 1, which represents how we tend to picture things, we come at the very end of an enormously long period of development. Sure, we know that human life takes up an incredibly small proportion of that line, representing a moment unbelievably thin. But *we* are what's going on NOW, and it's easy to think that we are what everything else has been leading up to. (Perversely, our sense of the enormity of past time can thus actually inflate our sense of self-importance in the larger scheme of things!) Because it skews things in

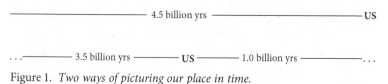

Figure 1. *Two ways of picturing our place in time.*

this way, our usual image of deep time is incomplete—not worthy of a culture that hopes to be scientifically literate.

The bottom part of the figure provides a more scientifically accurate picture of US in time. In reflecting on it, we are forced to think about the rest of the story: about the fact that those slow geological and biological processes we've been talking about will go lumbering on, generating new life changes in their wake, and certainly leaving US behind. Of course what follows US may for a time be some variation on the theme: who knows how long the human species will survive? But life may also take many new and interesting forms—dare I propose the possibility of more interesting forms?—in the next billion years.

2

First Among Unequals?

> We may be certain that the ordinary succession by generation
> has never once been broken, and that no cataclysm has deso-
> lated the whole world. Hence we may look with some confi-
> dence to a secure future of equally inappreciable length. And as
> natural selection works solely by and for the good of each being,
> all corporeal and mental endowments will tend to progress
> toward perfection.

Charles Darwin, *On the Origin of Species*

Charles Darwin's personal uncertainty as to the most fundamental
causes is very clear. In a letter to Asa Gray, his botanist friend at
Harvard, Darwin insisted that questions about the ultimate explanation of things are just "too profound" for the human intellect. The
origin of species is one thing; the origin of universes quite another.
"A dog," he wrote, "might as well speculate on the mind of Newton."

It is interesting to set this pessimistic-sounding assessment alongside my epigraph. Passages about the future are not plentiful in
Darwin's work. From this one, though, with its reference to "all
corporeal and mental endowments" tending to "progress toward
perfection," we might well infer that in his view ultimate things will
not *remain* too profound for Earthly intelligence. But what an optimistic sentiment it is! Indeed, many contemporary evolutionists in
science would find it rather too optimistic. What natural selection
counts as "good" in Darwin's sense here depends entirely on the
needs of creatures in the environments into which they are thrust,
and it isn't obvious that these must, in our future, include a
sharpening of human intelligence of the relevant kind. A deepened
capacity for theorizing in physics or philosophy probably wouldn't
increase the fitness of humans stuck on a planet decimated by

asteroids and facing another ice age. Furthermore, even if our species over time experienced improvements in "all corporeal and mental endowments," such improvements could well occur in fits and starts rather than in a steady upward march.

Having said that, we really have no idea what things will be like for humans on our planet in the distant future. Intelligent beings from our species or some other species may still be around—or around again—taking in the view a very, very long time from now. Darwin himself, we should expect, would be quick to acknowledge the Great Disparity. Thus the proper perspective, evolutionarily speaking, would appear to fall somewhere between the two Darwinian sentiments I have noted. We might charitably read Darwin's pessimistic comments to Gray in the present tense only, and so find space in his mind, all things considered, for the following view: Earthly mental life still has the mud of early evolution clinging to it. And as constituted at present, humans may be a long way from any capacity to realize insights on the most profound and complex matters. But who knows what the future may bring? Though from his time to ours it has remained no more than slightly ajar, let's call this "opening" for thoughts of deeper Earthly intelligence Darwin's Door—to the future.

THE TREE OF LIFE

Perhaps we can coax additional light through Darwin's Door by considering what serious science adds to the imagination on the matter of more highly developed mental powers. Let's start by getting the opinion of a distinguished contemporary Darwinian, the great biologist Christian de Duve.

De Duve spent much of his life adding to what we know about the cell, for which work he was awarded the Nobel Prize in 1974. Late in his career, he has turned his attention from the small to the large, taking on questions about the origin and evolution of life. In a 2002 article he had this to say: "If the tree of life goes on growing vertically, it could reach more than twice its present height. Extrapolating what has happened until now, this opens the possibility of mental powers that are simply unimaginable to our feeble means. This development could happen through further growth of the human twig, but it does not have to. There is plenty of time for other twigs to bud and grow, eventually reaching a level much higher than the one we occupy, while the human twig withers."

Toward the close of a video discussion filmed in 2005, three years after he wrote that article, a hale and hearty de Duve, 88 but clearly more than a match for the younger scientist interviewing him, returns to this point about how the future forces us to imagine unimaginable intelligence. The only difference, he says, between our brain and the brain formerly housed by the skull of "Lucy" (the famous 3.6 million-year-old *Australopithecus afarensis* fossil discovered the same year de Duve won his Nobel) is a three-fold increase in complexity. But think of Lucy trying to make sense of relativity theory, or painting in the Sistine Chapel. Then think, says de Duve, his face growing more animated, hands moving above his head, of possible beings thrown up by future evolution on our planet, with brains three times as large and complex as our own. Their mental experiences we cannot possibly imagine, just as Lucy couldn't possibly have imagined ours.

When the interviewer responds that this view sounds a tad optimistic, given the future developments it regards as likely or possible, de Duve is clearly incredulous. Sometimes optimism is warranted! Should we really suppose, on observing all that evolution has produced, noting the meandering but steady climb to greater complexity and the millions of years left to go, that there can be nothing more and nothing better than ourselves? "That's stupid!," he says, seemingly a bit uncomfortable at having to point it out, and the video promptly ends.

Should we agree? Is there a feasible—even if not inevitable—path into de Duve's sort of future? Might a visitor to our planet three million years from now find hominins with brains three times as large and complex as the human brain of today? As de Duve himself suggests, we can surely get at least part of the way to an affirmative answer by means of a simple inductive argument. Look at how evolution has operated in the past, continually producing new and fascinating beings—often ones more complex than had previously existed. Is this process just going to grind to a halt now that we have appeared? Hardly!

Clearly de Duve has in mind here the continuing operation of something we've had occasion to mention a time or two already: natural selection. It is important to see that with this mechanism, especially as clarified after Darwin through the development of genetics, we have a sharp and clear understanding of just *how* evolution has worked in deep structural and formative ways in the past and of how it can go on working far into the future.

Once this general point has been made, the point about the *extent* of the future can be brought back in to strengthen it. Indeed, there is so much time left that we may have a close parallel to the long past, in which despite many evolutionary switchbacks and setbacks, many circuitous routes and branching dead ends, a continuous path—indeed, a regular maze of pathways—leading ultimately to all the wonders of nature can in retrospect be discerned. We cannot be certain that the path will in similar ways take us to even higher and better and perhaps more interesting things moving forward in time, but there are strong grounds for supposing it very well may do so. And this modest conclusion is all I am after here.

A more specific version of the inductive argument beckons, too, grounded in what we know about *cultural* evolution. "What was extraordinary about human development," says Canadian author Ronald Wright in *A Short History of Progress*, "was that we 'leveraged' natural evolution by developing cultures transmissible through speech from one generation to the next." The results so far have certainly been impressive. From the wheel to the microchip, from early social arrangements to modern politics and government, *H. sapiens* has constantly been busying its large brain. Whether from fascination or need, through countless mild meanderings and the occasional quantum leap, this anomalous species has steadily transformed itself and its environment to the point where its members can be shocked to discover they are apes! As the evolutionary geneticist Jerry Coyne says, "we can fly above the tallest mountains, dive deep below the sea, and even travel to other planets. We make symphonies, poems, and books to fulfill our aesthetic passions and emotional needs. No other species has accomplished anything remotely similar."

Of course, on a less stirring note, we still behave like apes—and I mean the violent chimps, not the more peaceable bonobos—far too often. Looking into our species' past with the best science, we see not just how short but how violent and messy it is. There are many strands of beauty, too; our past has its deep insights, glittering deeds, and transcendent art. But it is a sad beauty, hemmed in by the ugliness of hatred and ignorance, and continually threatening to come undone. This side of human culture, one might say, provides a rather thin covering for our nakedness.

But all these observations, both uplifting and troubling, should in the present context only lead us to ask: if cultural evolution has brought us this far and is, as we all know, moving ever more rapidly in recent times (half of the developments Coyne cites occurred in the past century), what should prevent it from taking us much further still in the coming centuries and significantly enriching the achievements of our intelligence? Perhaps, stimulated by the challenges we presently face, important social technologies—such as sophisticated new forms of conflict resolution—will in time be added to our much-vaunted material ones, permitting the weave of beauty in our natures to become more visible.

Indeed, we're really just getting started, culturally speaking. Here again is Coyne, referring to the 6,000 years that have passed since the beginning of civilization, when cultural products seriously began to multiply: "This represents only one-thousandth of the total time that the human lineage has been isolated from that of the chimpanzees. Like icing on a cake, roughly 250 generations of civilized society lie atop 300,000 generations during which we may have been hunter-gatherers living in small social groups.... There's been relatively little time for evolutionary change since the rise of modern civilization."

When writing that last sentence, Coyne no doubt had in mind not just cultural evolution but evolutionary change through natural selection over the long periods that lie ahead. (Of course these two are importantly bound up with each other.) But by reference to cultural evolution alone, we can easily see how a large number of significant changes including ones relevant to the furtherance of our intellectual interests, such as a deepened collaboration, may come to be. If the species survives the present century—and even Sir Martin Rees gives us a fifty-fifty chance of doing so—it may have many new intelligent accomplishments to congratulate itself upon. And if we stretch the scenario out to 1,000 years after the present, the feasibility of serious cultural growth becomes even more obvious.

DE DUVE'S DESTINATION

But to get to the future envisaged by de Duve, we'll need to go further than a thousand years. And we won't do so unless human civilization can act its way through such dramas as the environmental one involving ice ages—the next installment of which may be beginning any century now. The past few million years have seen the glacial sheets regularly advancing and retreating, at a pace attuned to small but regular wiggles in Earth's orbit and spin that alter its orientation in relation to the Sun, diminishing slightly for a period of 100,000 years or so the amount of incoming solar energy. All past cultural activity and indeed the whole of human civilization has been squeezed into what many scientists think of as a time between ice ages, which, appropriately enough, is called an "interglacial." Will we and our descendants never be more than would-be actors, confined to this intermission in the drama?

Happily, the evidence is not entirely gloomy. For one thing, there's still a chance that the expected ice age won't arrive—our present humanly-influenced period of global warming may even enlarge that chance. But suppose it does. The distinguished human ecologist and future gazer Doug Cocks, on the basis of a very wide survey of expert opinion, judges that by means of such things as "domed cities, linear cities, underground cities, food factories, and giant green-houses," humans could comfortably manage the challenges posed by global cooling. Of course, providing for such comfort might itself be far from comfortable. But, like many others, Cocks judges that the relevant means are within our grasp and that the challenges are not insurmountable. In other words, it is possible that human civilization will survive and thrive despite the occasional descent of glaciers. (To a belief in this possibility even those who warn us of doom attest when, at the end of their books, they outline perhaps painful prescriptions and urge us to find the will to implement them before it's too late.)

Setting aside, then, the idea that glaciers will scrape hominins from the face of the Earth in the next few thousand years and looking further into the future, can we expect the continuing growth through natural selection of the human brain that de Duve's scenario requires? Scientists still don't know exactly what accounts for the surges in brain development that made a sapient *Homo* possible some 200,000 years ago. Perhaps it was the favoring, by natural selection, of ever more powerful variants of genes like microcephalin and the brain gene ASPM, known to affect brain-size. Perhaps it was natural selection operating on mutations involving what are called transposable elements, DNA segments that can move from place to place in the genome of a single cell. This is suggested by the respected molecular geneticist Roy Britten in a 2010 paper, "Transposable element insertions have strongly affected human evolution," published in the *Proceedings of the National Academy of Science.* However it happened in the past, there is some reason to think that natural selection will favor more brain development in the future.

Here cultural evolution may again play a role. As Nicholas Wade, author and science reporter for the *New York Times,* has written, "perhaps our distant descendants will be far more intelligent, having evolved in response to the ever increasing intellectual demands of a more complex society." Again: "Human brain size and intelligence have clearly expanded throughout most of evolution, and it would be strange if this trend should suddenly grind to a halt just as societies, and the skills needed to flourish in them, have become more complex than ever." Working in tandem, genetic evolution and such things as the complexity of our social structures and sophistication of our technologies—not to mention the need to meet and defeat complicated challenges to survival such as those already listed—could give a decided boost to hominin brain-power.

How much of a boost? Summarizing recent research in neurology, the well known Harvard psychologist Steven Pinker writes that general intelligence is correlated with (among other things) "the speed of information processing, the overall size of the brain, the thickness of the gray matter in the cerebral cortex, and the integrity of the white matter connecting one cortical region to another." How much more impressive might such things become? Might Darwin's dog yet probe the mind of Newton? More specifically, could brain development over a few million years more take humans as far past the brain we have right now as, over a similar period, we've moved beyond *A. afarensis*?

de Duve's affirmative view is supported by Simon Conway Morris, a distinguished British evolutionary paleontologist who is almost as strongly in favor of traditional Christianity as his colleague, Richard Dawkins, notoriously is opposed. According to Conway Morris, this sort of future development may indeed occur, but it may also represent the "upper limit," at least if we're talking about brains like ours: for various reasons including what recent studies are suggesting about "the limits of neurocomplexity," the brain could probably become only about "three times" as large and powerful as the one we have at the moment.

Only! Think of what such growth of the human brain would mean for human thought. All of our thinking has occurred within the single short stage of brain development we are presently in. This holds even if we say, with Wade and his sources, that the brain may have undergone some evolutionary chiseling since the origin of *H. sapiens* 200,000 years ago—perhaps as recently as 50,000 years ago, when modern behavior fueled by language may have had its origin. After all, systematic thinking in and about science, philosophy, and religion began far more recently than that. Any significant future developments of the human brain may consequently be expected to have a significant impact on how we think about such things.

To get some impression of how significant, let's return to our emphasis on cultural evolution, which it would of course be artificial to separate entirely from these natural processes. Think of how much knowledge and understanding would be generated if a truly big-brained species of the sort we are imagining were able to keep the cultural baton moving between generations for a million years or so—not an unrealistic thought given that it would have available to it all the lessons of past challenges overcome. (If these lessons were to bring with them success in the devising of artificial enhancements for the intellect of the sort dreamt of in the twenty-first century by so-called transhumanists and posthumanists, this point could of course be made even more emphatically, but there is no need to depend on such an intensification here.) Our own cultural baton, as we've seen, has been moving with any vigor for only about 6,000 years, an achievement we'd have to repeat more than 165 times to reach that million year mark.

I encountered Conway Morris's view about the tripling of brain capacity listening to the Gifford Lectures he delivered in Edinburgh in 2007 (one can do so online). These lectures were intended, as Gifford lectures generally are, to help tighten the connection between science and religion. It's interesting to see the idea of a superbrain of the future—Conway Morris calls the present occupants of our skulls "mere juveniles" by comparison—paired with a defense of traditional Christian ideas. One wonders whether something is being overlooked here.

However that may be, there is evidently sufficient reason, based on the history of the brain and realistic projections of genetic and cultural evolution into the future, to suppose that such a superbrain might yet come to be. The path from Darwin's Door to de Duve's Destination is one intelligence on Earth may well be taking in the next three million years.

BEYOND THE BRAIN

Three million years is a period that sounds incredibly extended. But as we saw in the previous chapter, it will be just the first of more than three hundred such periods, laid end to end, of fascinating new creative developments on Earth. Is there scientific support for the idea that these creative developments may include ones intentionally produced?

Here, where we're venturing to think of intelligent beings existing on our planet not thousands or millions but hundreds of millions of years after us, it is of course much harder to mark out a path from us to them, and our treatment is of necessity more speculative. But some things can be said with a fair degree of confidence even about times so distant. For one thing, thanks to Hutton's geological descendants, who have given us plate tectonics, we can say that an accurate office globe will look rather different in the year 100,002,013 than it does in 2013! And natural selection will continue to operate as the ages unfold, working with whatever materials the universe provides to fashion creatures great and small, and perhaps wise and wonderful, too.

What about the impact of such exceedingly rare events as the arrival of massive asteroids or the eruption of megavolcanoes? Might they too contribute to a redrawing of maps? Although worry about such things may seem unwarranted when we pass our minds across a few centuries or millennia, it becomes rather more realistic when considering periods as long as the one falling between the two dates mentioned in the previous paragraph. So we should assume that what we or any of our descendants would experience as utterly disastrous events will have occurred by the later of those dates.

But the significance of such events for the question whether intelligence has a *really* deep future on this planet is easy to exaggerate. This is nicely illustrated by a National Academy of Sciences colloquium on "The Future of Evolution" held in 2000. Scientists congregating for the event sounded pretty gloomy, citing numerous "declines of biomes and biotas." One might be forgiven for thinking there is no hope for naturally evolving intelligence on the planet in the distant future upon hearing it declared, in a subsequent report on their discussions, that "speciation in the large vertebrates is essentially over for the foreseeable future."

But of course the key word here is "foreseeable." As the author of the report admits, scientists at this colloquium were mostly concerned with the next 100 and the next 1,000 years. And the very next sentence of the report reads as follows: "Speciation may pick up again in the more distant future if isolated . . . populations are large enough and survive long enough to diverge, or if empty niches can be filled." It may even be that "numerous incipient species lie waiting as genetically differentiating populations after the last glacial phase and that, with time, they may produce a burst of originations."

Indeed, when scientists turn their gaze to the really deep future, they often sound quite optimistic. Robert Hazen, Professor of Earth Science at George Mason University, writes that "new great and wondrous beasts will inevitably evolve, in a geological moment, to fill those vacant niches. . . . Large mammals like ourselves may suffer mass extinction, but other vertebrates, maybe the birds, will take our place. Maybe penguins, which have recently been shown to evolve particularly rapidly, will morph and radiate to fill the niches: whale-like penguins, tigerlike penguins, and horselike penguins. Maybe the penguins will develop big brains and grasping fingers." One can imagine Hazen writing this with a smile, but only a glance at what we know about "morphing and radiating" in the past is required to see that these "maybes" reflect a sober truth.

The upshot is that new large vertebrates may appear again on Earth even if their evolution is slowed or halted in the near term. How long from now? The author of the National Academy of Sciences report mentioned above says it will only be after a very long time indeed— perhaps as much as a million years would need to have elapsed. (Hazen agrees with the million year figure, by the way.) But of course even a million years takes up only *one hundredth* of the period between 2013 and the year 100,002,013, and as we've seen, it is but one thousandth of the time that remains, in toto, for species capable of understanding themselves and the world—perhaps much better than we have done—again to evolve naturally on Earth. Thus even if we assume there is no feasible *unbroken* path from here to there, it is still a feasible possibility that intelligence like our own or greater than our own will in the extremely distant future have evolved on our planet through natural selection.

And that's just natural selection. What if we now reintroduce cultural evolution? Even if you thought I was being over-optimistic when, in the previous section, I spoke of a hominin species keeping the cultural baton moving for a million years, that *some* species will do so in a future sporting a thousand and more opportunities for such an accomplishment should seem an eminently realistic possibility. And perhaps the baton will be kept moving far longer than that.

In this context, where we are allowing our imaginations to range over much larger tracts of future time, it may be appropriate to bring into our discussion the ruminations of fourteen individuals—physicists, engineers, computer scientists, science fiction writers, doctors, and journalists—who are the contributors to a fascinating recent book called *Year Million*. It has been in keeping with my inclination to avoid the overly fanciful and stick with the realistic to set aside their speculations until now. But much that is unrealistic over even a million years' time may be quite realistic where we have as much as a billion years to work with. So how much more do these futurists think cultural evolution might produce, especially in intellectual terms?

Some of these writers emphasize, as I have done, how knowledge accumulated over hugely extended periods could be unspeakably greater than any we have acquired. Others entertain the idea of composite minds. There is of course talk of mind–machine interfaces. (Perhaps this is imaginable after the natural and cultural evolution of many millions of years, even if not, as the guru of transhumanism, Ray Kurzweil would have it, by 2050.) Still others speak of the "Universenet," a network of ultimate intelligence, or of the possibility that intelligence—or its alien products—might be shared with us from other planets. The projections one finds invariably involve *massive* increases in mental capacity.

Having traveled to de Duve's Destination and now also so far beyond, I suggest the report we file should reads as follows. Looking through Darwin's Door with the help of science, we see no limit to the possible development of intelligence in the deep future. Everything depends on what challenges intelligent beings encounter and the means they and natural selection find for dealing with them in the course of eons of time whose length we are hardly able to fathom. Given the many pathways from the present that we have charted, it is clear that a future with thoughts on profound things far more profound than our own is quite possible.

* * *

I suspect many evolutionists will think, at least initially, that by pushing at Darwin's Door in the ways I have in these first two chapters, drawing attention to the vastness of the deep future and the wonders it may hold in store, we are getting way ahead of ourselves. In certain parts of the world, including the rural area of Nova Scotia where I live, one can find reasons for sympathizing with such a view. For here even the deep past is still not acknowledged. Down the road from my old house, the local Baptist Church, whose handsome black and white steeple is excelled only by the sparkling blue ocean beyond, displays a message that people in 1883 who knew of Darwin's activities across the water would probably have welcomed: the church will receive a visitor this week from "Creation Ministries International." That's code for the intellectual ugliness of anti-evolutionism. Such messages, it might reasonably be thought, are signs that even science's work on the past amounts, so far, to no more than a half-revolution.

But while we labor to make that revolution complete, helping each other to imagine the deep past and to see how small changes over immense periods can, under the influence of such mechanisms as natural selection, add up to all the wonders of nature, we need to avoid skewing our overall picture by forgetting that the same basic equation (small changes + the right mechanisms for making use of them + immense periods of time = amazing results) is likely to have work to do in histories written about times to come. Reflecting today on what such histories may contain, we will find implications for human life and culture every bit as disruptive and important as those we are presently absorbing from the past. Indeed, the full scientific and cultural revolution we need will not have taken place until our imaginative gaze can take in the full panoply of Earthly time.

3

Evolutionary Skepticism

> There are many questions . . . which, so far as we can see, must remain insoluble to the human intellect unless its powers become of a quite different order from what they are now.
>
> Bertrand Russell, *The Problems of Philosophy*

> [Humans] plainly have the capacity to solve certain problems. It follows that they lack the capacity to solve other problems, which will either be far too difficult for them to handle within existing limitations of time, memory, and so on or will literally be beyond the scope of their intelligence in principle.
>
> Noam Chomsky, *Language and Problems of Knowledge*

It's hardly a secret that philosophers sometimes treat each other less than platonically in their symposia. In his memoir *The Making of a Philosopher* Colin McGinn memorably describes philosophical debate as "a clashing of analytically honed intellects, with pulsing egos attached to them." Philosophical discussion, he tells us, can be a kind of "intellectual blood sport."

McGinn, presently at the University of Miami, appears to take some pleasure in intellectual battle himself. He is often in print opposing this bit of shoddy thinking or that. But on one subject he himself has recently been put on the defensive, with many philosophers, including Daniel Dennett of Tufts University, the well known author of *Consciousness Explained*, arrayed against him. This is the question whether a solution can ever be found for the so-called "hard" problem of consciousness: the problem of how physical organisms like us can be subjects of experience.

McGinn's answer is no. Our minds have evolved to deal with more concrete worries than philosophical worries *about* minds. In his book *Problems in Philosophy* he extends this thought to a range of issues in metaphysics, the area of philosophy concerned with questions about what most fundamentally exists, and proposes CALM, which stands for "combinatorial atomism with lawlike mappings." Following out some suggestions made by Bertrand Russell and Noam Chomsky but also revealing the influence of Darwin, McGinn says that our minds have evolved to solve a certain sort of problem: one that can be CALMed by discovering the primitive constituents of things and principles governing their combinations. Most scientific problems fall into this category. But there are other problems that will not yield to the CALM approach. Conscious experiences, for example, which there is "something it is like to have," are not illuminated when thought of as aggregates of brain states, which there is "nothing it is like to have." Now, such problems might be solved easily by organisms that evolved differently in other possible worlds or in other parts of the actual world. But for us they are impenetrable, says McGinn: we just don't have the right concepts and capacities for dealing with them. "Progress would require us to overcome these architectural or constitutive limitations—which is not going to be possible without entirely reshaping the human mind."

Metaphysicians, as I've already suggested, have not taken kindly to being told they're just spinning their wheels! But McGinn's reasoning is exceptionally clear and penetrating. There is also a commonsensical quality to his basic idea, at least on the assumption that a Darwinian picture of our past is on the right track. We don't have any trouble understanding that spiders and fish and crows have evolved in such a way as to be good at certain things but not others. Why should we be any different?

I suggest we assume that McGinn is on to something, without committing ourselves to all the details of his account or regarding him as having justified more than doubt about the extent of our metaphysical powers. He himself calls CALM a "conjecture." Assume too that at least some of the beliefs people hold about how unCALM-able problems in metaphysics should be solved are therefore unjustified, unwarranted, unreasonable—use whatever expression picks out, for you, the condition of holding a belief when instead one should be skeptical or in doubt, believing nothing. Though McGinn doesn't express his intended contribution in quite these terms, this already explains to us how evolutionary thought can be seen as making room for skepticism.

But is it the whole story? In the present chapter, the first of a new pair of chapters aiming to expose the consequences for human inquiry of what we learned in the previous pair, I argue that it is not. In the next chapter we'll apply everything we've learned to religious and irreligious belief. (If you find the intricacies of philosophy difficult or—God forbid!—boring, feel free to skip over to that discussion after the first section here, which is particularly important, and thereafter dip into this chapter only as needed.) There is indeed a certain sort of "evolutionary skepticism" that can be developed as we stand at Darwin's Door gazing back into the deep past. But to get the complete version, and one that does not mislead, we will need to turn around and take in the deep future as well.

ESTABLISHING A BASELINE, OR WHY WE SHOULD JUST SAY NO TO GLOBAL SKEPTICISM

What sort of future-shock should we expect human inquiry to absorb? My suggestion, in brief, is that when we face the future, evolutionary skepticism will first be deepened and then lightened (perhaps in more than one sense, at least metaphorically: it may have an optimistic glint around the edges before we're through). It will be deepened because to our limitations, emphasized by McGinn, we will need to add the factor of our *immaturity*. This makes for a skeptical double-whammy of considerable force, which casts many of our treasured beliefs into question, showing them to be intellectually inappropriate to our place in time. But it will also be lightened because, having experienced a gestalt shift leading to a new conception of inquiry, we will imagine ourselves members of a trans-generational community that may together solve the deepest intellectual problems baffling us today—or the even more interesting problems into which they evolve. There's no guarantee of this, of course. But there's enough of a chance to make it reasonable for those with a deep love of truth to pursue inquiry in philosophy and science and other areas under such a conception, picturing their own contributions in the present rather differently than humans tend to do and certainly more modestly.

By thinking about such issues we enter another realm of philosophy—not metaphysics but epistemology. (Look it up and you'll find that it gets its name from the Greek word *episteme*, meaning knowledge.) Epistemologists think about the goals of inquiry and the extent to which our thought is fitted to achieve them. You might say that philosophers doing epistemology are thinking hard about thinking, before employing thought to examine other things.

If you survey philosophical history you'll find some epistemologists quite worried about a form of skepticism that is much more radical and all-consuming than evolutionary skepticism will turn out to be. Appropriately enough, it's called "global skepticism." The global skeptic questions the assumption that our cognitive faculties or processes of belief-formation are *reliable*—where reliability is a tendency to produce true rather than false beliefs. The ways of forming beliefs in question here include introspection, sensory perception, memory, and also rational intuition—the convenient process leading you to form the belief that all bachelors are unmarried just by thinking about its content, without doing a survey. Of course there are sources of belief other than these four, such as testimony and inference; the latter especially is of huge importance, since without deductive and inductive inference we could hardly develop our picture of the world very far. All these processes, says the global skeptic, may well be infected with unreliability, and so we shouldn't trust the beliefs they generate. We have no good reason to regard the beliefs produced by those faculties as true rather than false.

I could tell you a lot about why global skeptics have said such things, and about the general furor they often create in epistemological discussions. But instead I want to show why we needn't worry about global skepticism. I want to do so because when people first encounter epistemological questioning, they're sometimes inclined to throw up their hands in despair and say "So why should we believe anything?" Someone might say this even upon reading about evolutionary skepticism. I want to preempt this sort of reaction by addressing directly the idea that all our beliefs might be in trouble, showing how one can answer it, and then, having established a sort of baseline for our discussion, move on to consider the form of skepticism we *should* accept: evolutionary skepticism. That way, if anyone says "so why should we believe anything?" I can simply point back to this first section. That way, also, I might influence you to regard the results of my own skeptical argumentation, disheartening as they may seem, as not really so bad at all. Instead of the reaction mentioned above, I'll expect to hear: "Well, at least it's not global skepticism!"

I don't claim to have any way of proving the global skeptic wrong. The history of philosophy is littered with failed attempts to do so. But I do claim that there is a perfectly adequate alternative way of defusing the challenge here that anyone at all who wishes to inquire—to pursue the truth about herself and the world—can use. The thing to see is that we don't need to run from the global skeptic's suggestion. Indeed, let's start from there. Let's suppose we have no way of providing proof or evidence sufficient to justify the belief that our ways of forming beliefs aren't unreliable. This needn't trouble us because it is beside the point.

What is the point? *The point is that we really would like to know what the truth is, on a wide variety of issues and types of issue, and the belief-forming processes in question represent our only way of seeking it.* Somewhat more precisely and adequately: we desire to know the truth and the force of this desire is not cancelled by any other desire. How could it be? Satisfying other desires will require inquiry too—inquiry, for example, into how one might go about satisfying them. Moreover, at least at present, we have *only* the ways of pursuing the truth that are being challenged here. (This may be what the famous twentieth-century philosopher Ludwig Wittgenstein had in view when in his gnomic way he spoke of intellectual "hinges" which must stay put if the "door" of knowledge is to turn.) Notice also that the skeptic is unable to prove that our unavoidable belief-forming processes are *un*reliable. All things considered, then, we are quite reasonable in regarding those belief-forming practices as reliable for the sake of inquiry. We needn't even *believe* they are reliable—it's enough that we have good reason to take this idea on board mentally and act accordingly. Many philosophers will call this acceptance rather than belief.

Here's an analogy. Consider what counts as reasonable in our behavior when we really, really would like to win someone else's love (assume that this desire is not overridden by any other more important and conflicting desire). Do we need to have good evidence or proof that we'll be successful before it's reasonable to pursue such a thing? Do we even need to believe it? Clearly not. It's enough that there's a fairly decent chance we'll be successful and that we're willing to act accordingly. Similarly where the love of truth and understanding is concerned.

Some worries about belief may, however, remain. If we only accepted, in a nonbelieving way, that our intellectual processes are reliable instead of believing this, wouldn't we have to accept rather than believe their outputs too—the claims about the world or propositions they suggest as true? And yet those processes are called *belief-forming* processes. Precisely these belief-forming processes we're supposed to be defending against global skepticism. But my approach apparently doesn't allow us to do so.

One part of the solution to this puzzle, which anticipates a point I will be emphasizing later on, comes when we recognize that the evolution of *inquiry* could involve a transition from belief-forming to acceptance-justifying practices—at least on some of the issues generating an impulse to inquire. So long as for the present we can take for granted, as we seek the truth, what seems most probably true on the basis of inquiry already completed, and pass this along to the future, it may often seem a matter of indifference whether it is believed.

But another part of the solution—perhaps one more widely relevant—is this point: *it's completely impossible for humans to avoid forming at least some sensory, introspective, memorial, and rationally intuitive beliefs.* Regardless of what any skeptic has to say, we won't any time soon stop believing through introspection in the reality of certain mental events with our name on them, or through sensory perception in the reality of objects external to our mind. (Notice those trees outside your window? Try to stop believing that they exist.) Nor are we able to stop believing through memory in the reality of events falling into the past, or through rational intuition in the truth of certain mathematical, logical, and definitional propositions. Moreover, we inevitably venture beyond such beliefs to form at least some others via testimony and inference. Thus one answer to the question whether we should ever form beliefs if we only *accept* the general proposition that our belief-forming processes are reliable is that those processes are quite unavoidably spitting out beliefs during pretty much every waking moment. And if a belief is impossible to avoid, then it doesn't make sense to speak of replacing it with acceptance. Nor could one ever reasonably make it a requirement—something that "ought" to be the case—that we do so. As the eighteenth-century philosopher Immanuel Kant once said, quite atypically restricting himself to only a few words: "'ought' implies 'can.'"

You may wonder whether it really is impossible to cease believing. Can't we decide to believe things and also not to do so? This is indeed a common way of speaking, but it is misleading. All instances of believing are in an important sense involuntary. Beliefs are a bit like depression, coming over you or happening to you under certain circumstances, instead of being something that you do. You can of course do various things to try to make believing happen or cease. (If you doubt what I say, you can experiment by trying to overcome your doubt and choosing to really *believe* what I've said, just like that. Whatever happens, you'll see my point!)

To see more clearly why belief is involuntary, and at the same time why it is inimical to doubt or skepticism and also how it differs from what I've called acceptance, let's finish this section by looking a bit more closely at the nature of belief. William James pithily called belief "the sense of reality." If a child asks you "What's 2 + 2?" you will have the sense that the correct answer is "4." It just seems obvious; your rational intuition tells you it's true. To be of a mind to experience this reaction when such questions or similar stimuli arise certainly seems at least part of what's involved in believing that 2 + 2 = 4. Doubt or skepticism takes belief away precisely by removing that reaction.

Other philosophers have wanted to add other features, such as a disposition to act in accordance with what one senses as real. In their view, your belief that 2 + 2 = 4 exists only if you're also disposed to *say* that's how reality is configured, mathematically, and to act accordingly in other ways—perhaps by using that belief when figuring out what you owe in taxes. Still others hold that the neurons of your brain need to be humming this or that particular tune for you to be in a state of belief. Some philosophers will argue that you are absolutely sure of whatever you believe; others deny this.

All I want to insist on here is what most of these accounts—and also ordinary non-philosophical understandings of believing—will have in common: the view that believing something at least includes James's "sense of reality." A bit more precisely and accurately: it entails a disposition or tendency to have such an experience—an experience of its seeming that something is the case when that something comes to mind. (Why a disposition and not just intermittent experiences? To see why, notice that a moment ago while thinking about William James you believed that 2 + 2 = 4, even though the latter proposition was not then present to your awareness.)

That this Jamesian element is uncontroversially part of believing is enough to show belief's involuntariness, for you cannot manufacture a disposition like that at will. To do so would be something like feeling happy whenever you want to, just like that—psychologically impossible. You need evidence or something appearing as evidence (perhaps, as in the mathematical case, it will be self-evidence) in order to have the sense of reality. This means that someone who plans to believe anyway, even when the evidence looks unsupportive or even when she knows she hasn't examined it very carefully, is really advocating self-deception—something that both philosophers and non-philosophers can agree is problematic. Now, there is an attitude somewhat similar to belief that you can have voluntarily and despite lacking the sense of reality. It's what results from simply committing yourself to a position and acting accordingly. But that is indeed another thing—acceptance rather than belief.

It would be hard for inquiry to ignore belief altogether and always. For one thing, among the deepest aims of inquiry are knowledge and understanding, and these seem to entail belief. We are looking for a sense of reality that matches up in the right way with what *is* real. What's more, some really well-evidenced and obvious-seeming results of inquiry, as our excursus on the nature of belief confirms, may be impossible *not* to believe for careful inquirers, who keep their minds on evidence. And it may be natural and appropriate for us at this or that stage of human investigation, say in science, to mark off the more obvious-seeming things as belief-worthy. Not to do so might indeed be epistemically demoralizing. But what we've already learned is that at least on some matters inquiry can get along without belief. And we don't need proof or evidence for the basic assumption that our intellectual processes function reliably whenever beliefs *are* generated in order to reasonably accept that assumption and make use of those beliefs in the pursuit of truth. Recognizing these things provides a way of handling the fundamental epistemological questions raised by global skepticism, and shows why the evolutionary skeptic needn't worry about being bereft of all beliefs—left epistemically denuded on the path of inquiry.

HOW THE FUTURE CHANGES THINGS

In August 2012 the *New York Times* reported new fossil discoveries suggesting that "there were at least two contemporary Homo species, in addition to Homo erectus, living in East Africa as early as two million years ago." According to Fred Spoor, a paleoanthropologist at University College London and a member of the discovery team, research shows that "human evolution is not this straight line it was once thought to be." Indeed East Africa "was quite a crowded place, with multiple species." Bernard Wood of George Washington University, who was also involved in the discussion, responded to the new complexities created by the new evidence with a prediction about relevant inquiry: "By 2064 . . . researchers will view our current hypotheses about this phase of human evolution as remarkably simplistic." I thought to myself: "What about by 20,640?"

What *about* by 20,640—or 206,400 or 2,064,000? If we consider not just, with McGinn, how natural forces have limited our powers but also (as we saw in the previous chapter) how similar powers may be shaped and reshaped in the deep future as natural and cultural evolution go on, leaving us behind, is the result a significantly deeper evolutionary skepticism?

I want to suggest that it is, against the backdrop of my rejection of global skepticism. As we've seen, considerations available to us in the present do make belief rationally unavoidable or epistemically worthy in some cases, but the trick is to strike a proper balance between endorsing too much believing and endorsing too little. And it is precisely here that the deep future has something important to tell us. For it forces us to strike this balance differently than inquirers in philosophy and science and other areas of intellectual endeavor would otherwise be inclined to do.

With his reference to 2064 Wood may have meant to communicate the idea that more fully informed future scientists would be able to show those "current hypotheses" to be false. If so, perhaps he overstated his point. Surely, one wants to say, Wood doesn't know what will have happened by 2064—there might even be new evidence to confirm current hypotheses! Nonetheless, precisely because of our ignorance about the future of relevant inquiry, we would surely find plausible a weakened version of his point, which said only that researchers in 2064 *might* be able to show current hypotheses to be false.

This "might" captures what philosophers call "epistemic possibility." To say that a claim about the world, a proposition, is epistemically possible is roughly to say that even though it hasn't been established, *for all we know* it's true. Epistemic possibilities are claims we don't have any good reason to believe false, given our present evidence. For example, it is epistemically possible for you right now that you will become an evolutionary skeptic before you finish this chapter. It *might* be true! And you will have guessed by now that all the ideas about how things might go in the deep future dug up in earlier chapters count as epistemic possibilities. In the same way, the claim that the hypotheses referred to by Wood will be disproven by 2064 is epistemically possible: for all we know, this is true; we don't have any good reason to believe it false.

Notice that in the Wood case this is so because our body of fossil evidence may be considerably enlarged and the results of piecing things together considerably strengthened over time. Indeed, scientists in the relevant fields expect this to occur—the fossil evidence is still very spotty—and who knows what the results will be? This is fatal for belief of the relevant hypotheses, or at least for justified belief. And the concept of epistemic possibility allows us to show this with some precision. For if it's epistemically possible that those hypotheses will someday be shown false, then it's epistemically possible that they *are* false. We therefore (by the definition of epistemic possibility) have no good reason to believe otherwise—which is to say that we have no good reason to believe them true. Of course similar reasoning will show that we have no good reason to believe them false either, and so we are left in doubt about those hypotheses—the classic stance of the skeptic.

You may say that this is just a fancy way of talking about something evident to all of us already, quite independently of considerations about deep time or the Great Disparity. We don't need the latter notions to see that believing the current hypotheses of paleoanthropology would not be smart. That's just common sense. An alternative dismissal is more erudite. In philosophy of science there is the famous "pessimistic induction"—an argument inferring from past failures of theories in science that new failures involving our present theories will probably be noticeable in, say, one or two hundred years. Isn't my insistence that the future of science may outstrip the past simply recycling this idea?

Let me answer the second objection first. My arguments here will amount to something other than the pessimistic induction. For one thing, the deep future is not at issue in discussion of the pessimistic induction: although future changes are referenced, these are changes in the near future, and the basis offered for expecting them involves events occurring in the recent past. My skepticism has a different basis and also allows for much more general intellectual results than does the pessimistic induction. The story involving Wood, Spoor, and current scientific theories is for us only an example, and we might instead have focused on the metaphysical ideas impugned by McGinn. Forward-looking evolutionary skepticism, as I understand it, should deepen doubt in both areas, and for the same reasons.

As for common sense: what we said about Wood might indeed exemplify it. But that was just a warm up. What I want to show now is how similar reasoning, provided with a temporalist inflection, affects far more than just Wood's vulnerable-seeming hypotheses. We can see how the latter are vulnerable because we have limited evidence that may well be enriched. But in many areas, even evidence that seems to us much more substantial than the evidence available to paleoanthropologists should be treated in the very same way, because of what we have learned in the first two chapters of this book.

Take the scientific idea that there is genuine indeterminacy at the quantum level (the indeterminacy thesis). Or the philosophical view that true belief alone can never attain to knowledge. Or the political notion that democracy is the best form of government. Someone today who reflects on one of these claims may come to the conclusion that the preponderance of relevant evidence is on its side: unlike the paleoanthropological hypotheses we were just talking about, relative to a *large* body of evidence it is very probably true. Suppose that's the case. Still, I would suggest, the proper reaction might be not belief but skepticism because of an epistemic possibility of future refutation generated by our place in time.

But you may argue back: if, say, the indeterminacy thesis is very probably true, then we can infer that very probably there's no hidden argument showing it to be false. (For if it's true, then *that* has to be true as well.) But if it's very probable that there's no hidden argument showing it to be false, then surely it's reasonable to believe this and we no longer have an epistemic possibility of the sort that, as we saw in the Wood case, is enough to remove the reasonableness of belief. We've blocked all paths to the view needed here: that it's epistemically possible that the indeterminacy thesis is false and thus unreasonable to believe it true.

This is a tempting way of reasoning, but two things make it unsuccessful: a confusion of probability on available evidence with degree of justified belief, and the basic facts about our place in time. Even if, relative to a certain body of evidence, a claim is very probable, it doesn't follow that it is *believable*. To see this, consider the following scenario. Suppose you have no familiarity with the game of basketball and in particular no clue how difficult or easy it is to shoot free throws. Suppose also that you know some stranger is going to shoot 1,000 free throws. You then observe her make two of the first three shots. How probable is it that she will make her 1,000th free throw? Relative to the evidence you have so far, the probability of that proposition being true is 2/3. In spite of that, the belief that she will make that final free throw is not justified. Yes, you are justified in believing that the proposition in question is probable on your evidence. But you have insufficient evidence to believe that it is *true*. Why? Because the chance that new evidence will undermine your current evidence is just too high (perhaps the stranger will miss her fourth free throw). In other words, belief is not justified here because you ought to have serious doubts about whether your current evidence is representative of the total evidence. Suppose, however, that later on you see the stranger make 200 of 300 free throws. Then even though the probability that she will make her 1,000th free throw has not changed—it is still 2/3—the epistemic status of the belief that she will make her 1,000th free throw has changed. That belief is arguably now justified, partly because you have good reason to think that the evidence you have is representative of the total evidence.

Similarly, even if our present evidence makes the indeterminacy thesis (or one of the other claims I mentioned) very probable, we still have to ask whether our current evidence is representative of all the evidence that's out there. If our situation may, for all we know, be that of the person who has seen three free throws rather than that of the one who has seen 300, then we should be in doubt about whether our evidence is representative of the total evidence—whether the latter *too* favors our claim rather than containing a decisive refutation. And if we have to be in doubt about this, well, then we have to be in doubt about whether that claim is true.

I've introduced a new phrase here: "total evidence." By this I just mean everything in the world, whether accessible to us or not, that bears on whether some proposition is true. We can't reasonably think of a claim as accurately portraying what is the case if we can't reasonably regard the total evidence in this sense as supporting it. For if a claim is true, then the total evidence supports it. That's just a logical fact. Rational intuition will help you to see it. Nonetheless— perhaps in part because we've failed to take the long view afforded by deep time—it is one very commonly overlooked by philosophers, who commonly use the phrase "total evidence" to refer to total *available* evidence. From now on let's use the upper case "T" and "E" to distinguish my truly all-inclusive concept from theirs: Total Evidence. Given what we've just seen, if we have to be in doubt about whether the Total Evidence does support a proposition, because of the epistemic possibility that it doesn't, then we also have to be in doubt about whether that proposition states what is the case.

But surely it would be laughable in many cases to deny that we *do* have to be in doubt about what the Total Evidence shows, precisely because of our present primitivity and what may in the deep future be revealed about the composition of that evidence. In many cases there's just too big a chance that we're in the situation of the person who has only seen three free throws out of a thousand.

We need to do two things now: first, strengthen this claim, and second, try to get clearer about how widely it may be applied. How exactly does our place in deep time support such a claim, and how can we strike the "tricky balance" mentioned above, distinguishing those claims affected by it from those that are not? The following two sections address these tasks.

THE IMMATURITY OF THE SPECIES

If someone calls you immature, it's a good idea to check whether they mean this *descriptively* or *evaluatively*. If the former, they're only saying that, in some respect, your capacities are not as fully developed as they may be in the future (perhaps you've just started playing chess and are being compared with a chess master). There's no suggestion that something's wrong with you. But if the latter, they're saying that you are less than sensible or appropriate in your behavior or in the management of your emotions—that you are in this way less fully developed than might be expected or desired. Now the suggestion *is* that something's wrong with you. Intended descriptively, "She's very immature" is not a criticism; intended evaluatively, it is!

Human beings at our present stage of development may legitimately be described as intellectually primitive or immature in *both* senses, and both kinds of immaturity often contribute to a justified doubt, in contexts of inquiry, as to whether our evidence is representative of the Total Evidence. At the end of the last chapter we were talking about the first sort of immaturity: our present immaturity in the descriptive sense. But this awareness can now be enriched. For the human species is also immature in the *evaluative* sense. Not only might there be a huge differential, in terms of intellectual capacities and achievements, between where we are and where we'll arrive, but we've done less well than might have been hoped with the time we've already had. A small example is provided even by McGinn's comment about "intellectual blood sport." The violence still so much a part of our social lives bleeds into inquiry too: philosophers fight, theologians fight, political commentators fight, even scientists fight—though admittedly collaboration has made more headway in science than in many other areas. And often it is our burning "sense of reality" that is to blame. Of course, if evolutionary processes of the sort to which McGinn appeals are alone responsible for this immaturity, then we can't really berate ourselves for not having reached a more fully developed intellectual condition than the one we presently display. But we certainly may wish that we had!

So how is this two-sided immaturity relevant epistemically? It won't be difficult to see how. As we internalize the deep future it's with the realization that there's just an incredible amount of time left for amazingly complex intellectual developments utterly contrary to present views to be achieved, even if progress is incremental or interrupted, and also that we haven't even used the very short time we've had especially well, and so may have missed a lot of things that might have caused views contrary to our own to be formed. A deep time perspective on inquiry, in which we trade our human timescales for those of the universe, should have a decided impact. In particular, it's going to seem rather plausible that it might take a lot longer for human intelligence to get anywhere really interesting than we had thought. Many deep layers of matured thought, developed only after much difficult collaboration over unbelievably long periods of time, may need to be laid down before we are in a position to see the deep truth of things (if we ever are). Thinking in terms of seventy years, a few human lifetimes, or even in terms of centuries—all is arbitrary. Why suppose that the universe of knowledge is calibrated to our timescales? It might well be otherwise. We would be rash indeed to deny it.

Someone may now suggest, with specific reference to science, that it doesn't follow from the fact that things in our universe happen slowly, over enormous tracts of time, that the process of discovering the truth about these processes must be equally slow. This thought is correct. It's true that scientific theorists may have already discovered all the most important physical facts at the very beginning of inquiry, and that for ten million centuries beyond the twenty-first our descendants will simply glorify us for our achievements. But is it reasonable to *believe* this? If we have chosen to pursue truth and understanding, we have to assume that the truth and understanding we seek are possibly attainable, and also that efforts to attain them made so far are not altogether without value. We will thrill to the adventure of the quest and love the idea of ideas capable of ramifying down the centuries, world without end. But if we have taken the measure of the Great Disparity, we will also admit that even where we have done our best, many of our efforts to understand the universe, and many efforts expended before us, may in fact lead to a variety of intellectual dead ends; or may generate insights much smaller than we had wished, to be relativized by insights of the future; or may have produced only small stepping stones to genuine insight, which awaits us in distant times to come. Much as a discerning younger brother will be ready for his much more experienced older brother to poke holes in his science project, so, if we have truly taken in the billion years that may await the activity of Earthly intelligence, we will be ready to have the primitivity of our efforts made manifest by those who come after us. (That is the burden of being early!) We will reconcile ourselves to sometimes—perhaps often—being the pioneer Moses, wandering in the wilderness, instead of Joshua, who actually enters the promised land.

Notice that a different relation to time and a different history of intellectual effort and achievement than our own would yield a much weaker argument for evolutionary skepticism. If we were an old species, with not just 6,000 but 60,000 or 600,000 years of inquiry behind us, and if the record of that process of inquiry showed a long period of development and change in our thinking on relevant matters and then a slow leveling off and convergence of views, maintained over thousands of years despite the most careful scrutiny, things might be different. Even if we were a young species inheriting such matured results from species that came before, arguably it would *not* be epistemically possible for us that much more development will be required to see the truth on important matters or that yet more capable and mature and fully informed minds will, 10,000 or 100,000 or 1,000,000 years after us, definitively show that the indeterminacy thesis is false or that true belief alone can be knowledge or that democracy is not the best form of government. Things could indeed be different. But, as they are, evolutionary skepticism flourishes.

THE TRICKY BALANCE

What I've been suggesting is that reflection on the immaturity of the species gives shape and substance to a new form of skepticism—or, perhaps better, to a completed version of evolutionary skepticism. Because we are immature, belief is often premature. But how widespread should this skepticism be? Can we say anything more precise about the area of propositional space over which it holds sway? We know already that it's not the entirety of propositional space, and also why. In the last sections we saw that some beliefs are naturally unavoidable and others rationally unavoidable. (Perhaps contemplating the powerful and deeply interwoven strands of evidence we have for some claims—that natural selection has occurred? that time is deep?—will leave us unavoidably believing that we're in the "300 free throw" position even after taking into account our place in time.) We also have reason to link evolutionary skepticism to certain specific examples, such as the indeterminacy thesis. But it would be nice to have some criteria for discerning the *types* of beliefs that are vulnerable here. I think much more work may be required to deal with this issue fully and satisfactorily. But as an opening move I will suggest a criterion that may legitimately be applied (though I don't claim that it's the only one).

This criterion refers to properties some beliefs possess and others lack. Notice, first of all, that a belief one is inclined to form may be *precise* as opposed to vague: its content is clearly specifiable. A belief candidate may furthermore be *detailed* as opposed to simple, full of particulars and thus complex or multifaceted, having many parts. Third, it may be *profound*. Profundity in a belief, let's say, involves its offering a deep understanding of how things are in the world, and one fairly comprehensive in scope. (Thus the belief that everything is material in nature is in this sense profound but the belief that there are three hundred and sixty three pebbles on my driveway is not.)

Three further properties, more "external" than the three already listed and having to do with how humans are related to the content of a belief, may be added. For a belief may also be *attractive*—such as human beings generally would wish to be true. It may be *ambitious*, by which I mean that it may concern matters that strongly resist human attempts to understand, perhaps even where evaluative immaturity has been overcome. (This is where McGinn's work again has relevance.) Finally, a belief may be *controversial*, with different diligent inquirers finding different and conflicting views on it persuasive.

Most of these are "degreed" properties, by which I mean that beliefs may feature more or less of the things referred to. And my suggestion is that where they are present in a high degree and overlapping—that is, where a candidate belief exhibits *all of them at once*—a diligent inquirer will be prevented by the recognition of this fact from forming the belief. I would also propose that where *most* of them (i.e. four or more) are present, belief formation will *typically* be prevented—that is, will be prevented except in the most unusual circumstances, in which a belief can make a strong case for itself despite initial appearances. Again, I don't claim that my property-based criterion is the only one that will work. Nor do I deny that some individual beliefs may intuitively be judged skepticism-worthy by reference to our immaturity even though no such general criterion has been applied. Finally, I do not claim that it reflects a *necessary* condition of doubt-worthiness (such that even though this criterion has not been applied to the individual beliefs just mentioned, it must be one we *could* apply with the same result). All I claim is that it represents a *sufficient* condition of doubt-worthiness.

Think about it: a precise and detailed belief has many alternatives—there are always going to be many ways things could be other than the precise and detailed way it proposes, and so just as many ways we could go wrong in holding it. This may not bother us if we are dealing with fairly local and manageable matters, such as pebbles on driveways, but what if we also have profundity? A profound belief that is precise and detailed may have an *enormous* number of alternatives, including many we have not noticed.

And now the connection to the deep future starts to emerge. For, having internalized deep time, we will often think to ourselves: If we may be just at the beginning of the flowering of intelligence on our planet, will the evidence we have been able to gather and assess so far come anywhere close to encompassing all those alternatives? In such cases one should certainly start to wonder whether evidence turned up only in the deep future will show to be true one of the alternatives to the precise, detailed, and profound belief we are contemplating.

But suppose now that the belief in question is not just precise, detailed, and profound—it's also attractive, ambitious, and controversial. I'm guessing you can see where this is going! Because of our evaluative immaturity, relevant to attractive beliefs may be opposing evidence that humans are prone to *neglect* because we want those beliefs to be true. Ambitious belief-candidates we should be especially willing to let go in light of the future, because of our immaturity in the descriptive sense: since they concern matters that resist human intelligence, we will reasonably hope that the development over much time of more subtle capacities or the fuller maturing of our own limited present capacities will allow a more confident view on the problems they purport to address. And where there is controversy, there are respectable intellects drawn to quite different beliefs. (In contemporary epistemology, this issue of peer disagreement looms large, but notice that in the present context it is just one of several factors that together may lead us to conclude that the future disagreement of more fully enlightened epistemic *superiors* can't be ruled out.) To wrap things up, where most of these six properties are combined and to a high degree— on that class of beliefs—we should be prepared to stamp the word "vulnerable" instead of "safe." And where *all* appear, belief should be regarded as premature and inappropriate.

Notice how this criterion can be applied to explain why Wood was right to be concerned about the future. Those current hypotheses in paleoanthropology are precise and detailed and also have a considerable degree of profundity. They score lower on attractiveness and ambition, perhaps, but high again on controversy. The indeterminacy thesis and the views McGinn addresses are also represented here. Current views about the nature of the mind, for example, are often quite precise and detailed, as well as profound. They are also very controversial and, of course, ambitious. In the next chapter we will find that more views still—including some very much taken for granted by most of us—fall prey to the new skepticism.

It's also worth noting that our criterion can do all this work without affecting any of my own arguments—or the scientific claims on which they are based. Remember that I need only epistemic possibility for the scientific propositions I'm using, and that affirming this is compatible with skepticism about those propositions. None of the other premises of my reasoning is subject to our criterion either. In particular, the claim *if the denial of a proposition is epistemically possible for us then we are unreasonable in believing it* is true by definition, and belief of it is certainly not profound or attractive, ambitious or controversial. And the claim *if a belief exhibits precision, detail, and profundity, as well as attractiveness, ambition, and controversiality then its denial is epistemically possible for us at our stage of inquiry* is not controversial—at least not yet! Of course whether belief of this claim will be or remain controversial only time will tell. It is certainly not ambitious or generally attractive. Nor is it profound. (Notice that though epistemological, this belief does not seek to answer theoretical questions in epistemology which might well be regarded as participating in the profound, such as questions about the nature of knowledge. No comprehensive or deep picture of the nature of reality is here put forward. Rather we have something more like the view that it's too early to put such pictures forward with any confidence.) Similar reasoning will show that other claims lurking in the background of my main argument are likewise untouched by our criterion. And the inferences I have used are all simple deductive inferences; the belief, of any one of them, that it is valid will lack all of the properties mentioned except, perhaps, for precision and detail.

But even if it turned out that belief of my criterion was unjustified *by that criterion*, there would, paradoxically, be no insurmountable problem for my view, since (as was earlier suggested) it might function perfectly well in philosophical inquiry even if accepted rather than believed. Indeed, what we may come to accept at a certain stage of inquiry, perhaps on the basis of claims and inferences themselves cautiously accepted, is that we should not believe!

Much more could and should be said about all these matters. But perhaps this outline will suffice to bring the shape of a completed evolutionary skepticism into a better focus, and reveal even more clearly how much the future should matter in epistemology.

AN EPISTEMIC SILVER LINING?

I want to conclude this chapter by exposing a bit more fully what a full-blooded evolutionary skepticism means for epistemology. It's not all bad! You may have found some of the results of previous sections intellectually deflating, but considered from the right perspective they can appear exciting and liberating instead. As mentioned earlier, evolutionary skepticism is not just deepened but also lightened when we fill it out using temporalist ideas—looking both into the deep past and into the deep future. How can this be?

The key is to allow temporalist thinking to push us all the way over into a new way of conceiving the human investigative task, which pictures things *diachronically* (spread out over time) instead of *synchronically* (at a time). We need to see our role in the perhaps greatly extended processes of inquiry differently, thinking about what intellectual goals and attitudes short of the ultimate attainment of knowledge and understanding should, at least on some difficult matters, give life to inquiry when we may be near the beginning of the process. (Perhaps the "sense of reality" that comes with belief will often only make it harder to keep our place in time clearly in focus.) Evolutionary skepticism arises within inquiry, and is indeed part of an attempt to further discovery of truths about the world by means compatible with our present primitivity. If it tells us certain beliefs are off limits, inappropriate to our time, it will also tell us how, by transitioning to acceptance and in many other ways, we can become epistemically *reoriented*. Of course if what seems most important to us is that we figure everything out, as swiftly as possible, then such a reorientation may not seem very attractive. But if we allow our imaginations to linger in the thought of an understanding of the world beheld by finite beings but so magnificently deep that all our present thinking, even if it contains much truth, is just the tip of the proverbial iceberg, we may be attracted to a different stance. We may think that it would be inestimably good if this thought were true, or could become true, and may want to do what we can to help ensure that it does become true.

McGinn doesn't have much time for the idea that the future might change things. Mentioning in passing the idea of a million years of further investigation, he ventures another conjecture: that nothing will change and we will still be baffled by our minds. But I wonder whether he has really got deep time "in the gut." Sure, it's epistemically possible that he's right, but I'm more interested right now in the clear epistemic possibility that he's wrong, and the new agenda for epistemology that is lurking nearby. For even if our thoughts are now limited in the ways McGinn suggests, why suppose that this will always be the case, if through a future with a hugely intricate inter-weaving of evolutionary factors beyond our fathoming, the human mind adapts to new circumstances, some determined by the rest of nature and some of its own making? Our social lives, as noted in the previous chapter, are only now becoming at all sophisticated. Who knows what new environments we will need to adapt to in the future, and what new mental structures will be fashioned by natural selection—in our brains or in others to whom the intellectual baton is passed? Taking limitation and our deep immaturity *together* changes things.

The thought of early cartographers that the edge of the continent and the Pacific would be found just over the American Appalachians was put into perspective by the vast plains and much more formid-able Rockies lying beyond. Thinking that the end of our most ambi-tious intellectual projects can clearly be seen from the intellectual peaks we have scaled so far seems similarly naive. If we really have just begun the processes of intellectual investigation and if as much as a billion years for inquiry may remain, shouldn't we reckon that some of these problems may well be solvable over perhaps hundreds or thousands of generations to come, instead of in our own lifetime or a few more? May not some of the most profound projects of human intellectual exploration indeed properly be viewed as projects for the *species as a whole*?

Evolutionary skepticism not only results in the loss of many of our present beliefs but bids us find this thought and savor it.

4

The New Pessimism

My mind is not closed, as you have occasionally suggested, Francis. My mind is open to the most wonderful range of future possibilities, which I cannot even dream about, nor can you, nor can anyone else. What I am skeptical about is the idea that whatever wonderful revelation does come in the science of the future, it will turn out to be one of the particular historical religions that people happen to have dreamed up.... [I]f there is a God, it's going to be a whole lot bigger and a whole lot more incomprehensible than anything that any theologian of any religion has ever proposed.

Richard Dawkins to Francis Collins, in a *Time* Discussion

"Yes!" I said to myself when I read this comment. "An evolutionist who recognizes that evolution isn't just about the past!" The comment came at the very end of a recent debate, convened by *Time*, between the famous biologist Richard Dawkins and the former director of the National Human Genome Research Institute Francis Collins, an evangelical Christian. Acknowledging a "most wonderful range of future possibilities," Dawkins had come close to noticing what the deep future means for religion.

But it was not to be. The debate ended precisely where it might most fruitfully have begun. Though Dawkins appeared to be gazing through Darwin's Door, it was apparently still with vision obstructed by the smoke of battles between science and traditional religion—battles that have helped turn many scientists into metaphysical naturalists, who believe not only that science must appeal exclusively to natural causes (this is known as methodological naturalism) but that physical nature, as progressively exposed to us by science, *is the only reality*. As one can see on looking closely—and this interpretation is borne out by everything else he has had to say on the subject—

Dawkins had no "stage two" of discussion on science and religion in mind as he ended his debate with Collins. His mind appears quite closed to the existence of an extra-scientific reality: future revelations are, for him, restricted to the "science of the future." Though of course he admits that our understanding of its laws may change, Dawkins believes that there is nothing more to reality than the law-abiding world of physical nature explored by science.

This belief undergirds what I'm going to call the "old pessimism" about religious belief. Many of religion's critics today are metaphysical naturalists. And if metaphysical naturalism (hereafter, naturalism) is true, then religious beliefs are not. But there is a *new* pessimism, which, as I want to show in this chapter, stems from the evolutionary skepticism we've just been discussing. This new pessimism is not just an alternative to the old. If it applies at all, it *consumes* the old: naturalistic belief and the quite general irreligious belief it entails are as subject to evolutionary skepticism as anything else.

After getting a bit clearer, in the brief opening section of this chapter, about some of the religious notions we'll be needing, I want to address directly how the old pessimism is overtaken by the new. Then, in the heart of the chapter, I will set out some more general evolutionary arguments opposing both religious and irreligious belief (and indirectly opposing naturalistic belief)—arguments for evolutionary religious skepticism.

"RELIGION" AND RELATED IDEAS

As was mentioned in the Prologue, you'd have to travel almost all the way through the history of the planet, stopping just 50,000 years or so short of the present, to meet beings both anatomically and behaviorally like us, ready to undertake religious rituals. What's more, you'd have to make it almost all the way through that 50,000 year span of time to arrive at religious movements with ripples reaching our shores: they are most noticeable during what writers have called the "Axial Age," a pivotal period lasting from about 2,900 to 2,200 years ago, in which, among other things, Taoism, Confucianism, and Buddhism made their appearance. And of course, Christianity, Islam, and certain other religious traditions of influence today come even later.

With that potted history, I accomplish several things. One, I introduce a conception of religion according to which we should think of it as spread out over much time instead of—as is far too common—only in terms of how it appears at *this* time, in the present (a diachronic conception instead of a synchronic one). Two, when combined with what we have seen about the deep future, it allows me to make my point about temporal contextualization in specifically religious terms: think of how recently religion arose! think of the few thousand years it has had against the possibility of a billion! But, three, I can also deal with the question of what I mean by religion.

For we all understood what was said in that potted history. We all know what sorts of rituals, undertaken in hunter-gatherer societies, count as religious; and I'll bet no one was surprised that the traditions I mentioned were called religious. Indeed, we are all able to identify many examples of human religion, in its various manifestations over time. (How much disagreement would there really be?) So there is enough common knowledge on the subject for us to understand well enough what I mean when I say that by the prospects for religious insight I mean the *prospects for thinking of the sort that is character-istic of human religion as thus identified.*

Such thinking, as is well known, includes ideas about things tran-scendent to—more than, deeper than, greater than—the world of mundane events, whose autonomy scientific critics of religion are aiming to defend. (Sometimes this notion of transcendence is con-strued so narrowly as to be restricted to person-like gods or God: it's important to note that an emphasis on such enhanced personhood may be sufficient for religiousness but it is not necessary.) Whether in terms of the spirit in all things or gods or goddesses or an all powerful Creator or the Buddha-nature or the one reality Brahman or the Tao, religion throughout our history has seen itself as putting us in touch with higher realities than those of mundane life or the sciences that have proved so clever at charting its regularities. These allegedly higher realities are regarded as capable of benefiting us in distinctive ways, and precisely because they are viewed as higher and greater than mundane realities, the benefits flowing from them are typically regarded as higher and greater than mundane benefits, too.

Let us therefore take religious belief to encompass all states of believing that are expressible by a proposition entailing that there is some such trans-mundane reality. (To say that a belief is expressible by a proposition means that were someone to ask you what you believe on some matter, your answer could be given in the form of a proposition: for example, I believe that *Obama will be President from 2012 to 2016*. And to say that one proposition entails another means it's impossible for the first to be true unless the second is true also. Thus *Obama will be President from 2012 to 2016* entails that *someone will be President in 2013*.) Irreligious belief—or religious disbelief, as we might also call it—I will regard as including all states of believing expressible by a proposition entailing that there is no religious reality of any kind. Religious and irreligious belief, in a sense of "belief" that includes what I emphasized in the previous chapter, are of course very common. Those who believe that reality includes God or some other transcendent thing are disposed to have experiences in which this just seems to be the case. Something similar is true for someone who says there is no Divine reality of any kind. That is how she sees the world: if you get her to put away that crossword puzzle and contemplate metaphysics, she'll tell you so.

Notice that, given these definitions, the belief that this or that *particular* religious proposition is false—the belief, for example, that Zeus does not reign atop Mount Olympus or that there is no being who is omnipotent, omniscient, and perfectly good—does not yet count as irreligious belief, for it does not entail the denial of *all* religious propositions, and so despite anything said here might escape evolutionary skepticism. Indeed, a certain traditional form of atheism may be in better shape, evolutionarily speaking, than either the traditional theism it denies or any more general denial of all religious claims. But of course Dawkins and others among the so-called "new atheists" are not just atheists in that limited sense. They are full-blooded *irreligious believers* and also metaphysical naturalists, and they typically are the former because they are the latter. Precisely this, as we need now to observe more closely, is what makes their belief untenable in an age of temporal contextualization.

WHY THE OLD PESSIMISM IS PREMATURE

People like Dawkins have a very special place in their hearts for nature. They are in awe of the power of science to reveal its structure, one chisel stroke at a time, and greatly admire the truth-seeking commitment of the best among the world's scientists. Feelings of depth, for them, will likely prominently include the sort that led Einstein to pen these words: "What I see in Nature is a magnificent structure that we can comprehend only very imperfectly, and that must fill a thinking person with a feeling of humility. This is a genuinely religious feeling." In Einstein's stretched sense of the word, Dawkins has said, he is religious, too. Note the upper case "N" Einstein uses for the word "nature," and also his use of the word "structure." Here again we have the scientist's love of orderliness and harmony in the natural world, whose laws he or she is seeking more fully to comprehend.

If now we introduce traditional religion into the discussion, we will make many Nature-loving scientists bristle. At the end of the passage just quoted, Einstein adds the following thought: "The idea of a personal God is quite alien to me and seems even naive." And in a letter recently made public, the great physicist calls the religion of the Bible "pretty childish." Dawkins' antipathy to God and gods is of course well known.

This reaction of many scientists, and many of those influenced by science, is elicited not just by religion's suggestion that their picture of the world, with its simplicity and harmony, needs to have colored into it or over it a radically distinct dimension of reality, not similarly ordered and available to empirical inspection (though I suspect this is often a factor). What really irritates, it seems, is conventional religion's very unscientific tendency to appeal to authority instead of evidence when talking about this distinct dimension, and to cover up for inadequacies revealed in some of the struggles between science and religion with defensive bluster.

Religion, as construed by a writer like Dawkins, is full of excessive credulity, wishful thinking, dogmatic preaching, attempts at brainwashing, and lack of investigative zeal. Just look at it! 150 years after Darwin, as I noted in a previous chapter, much religion is still stubbornly opposed to evolution. What it wants to add to science's magnificent picture are the awkward crayon marks of a child. No wonder, then, that religion should be regarded as an enemy. Within the context of evolutionary thought, it can be tempting to regard religion as an early aberration and to see science as alone representing the way forward. Many give in to this temptation, insisting that religion should be shed like a snakeskin.

Such resistance to religion is often quite understandable; in some contexts it is even admirable. But because of the love of Nature I have noted and a commitment to science, conjoined with their tendency to associate religion strictly with cultural phenomena that are giving science a hard time, writers like Dawkins and Christopher Hitchens and others are prevented from noticing some rather important ways in which evolution and religion might be thought connected. It is somewhat surprising to see champions of truth and rational investigation so incurious about the idea that there might be more to reality than is available to twenty-first-century science and its imaginable descendants. This idea seems to be the victim of guilt by association (the association being with crass traditionally religious portraits of reality and their crassest defenders). But the rejection of religion of all kinds, conceived or unconceived, on account of the infirmities of much present religion is simply an error—and an evolutionary one at that.

Let's develop this point just a bit further. The proper critique of naturalism and a perfectly general irreligion will emphasize evolution not less but *more*. Why say, for example, as in the Prologue we saw Hitchens do, that the religious life of the world as we have it today marks the infancy of the species instead of allowing that it might mark the infancy of religion? If you assume that the prevailing religious "isms" represent the only forms of religious thinking the world will ever know, then upon observing their failure, you will indeed infer that religion is brain-dead. But such an assumption is disallowed by a properly evolutionary perspective. An evolutionary perspective should sensitize us not just to happenings in the distant past but also to the possibility of a hugely extended future, with eons left for human beings to think, perhaps more fruitfully, about ultimate things. Sure, it could be that nothing more impressive than current religious thought will ever be known. And even if that's not how things turn out, it could be that new ideas will come with a completely new way of conceiving reality, one that no longer divides it into the "natural" and the "supernatural" in the way we often do. But these things are quite consistent with future intellects on the basis of deeper insights than our own affirming the existence of dimensions of reality that could not be reached through any continuation of inquiry into its law-governed dimensions, no matter how far extended.

This is where the nasty details that Dawkins and others have dug up about the past life of religion can actually be helpful to an evolutionary critic of their views. I will not recite the litany of grievous errors and shameful moments in the past religious life of humans; most readers of a book like this will know it by heart. Suffice it to observe that any aspiration humans may presently have for religious insight cannot be helped by the sins of past religion. How do we know that those sins have not left us severely impaired in relevant respects? Who can say what burning a thousand women as witches or decapitating a thousand infidels does to deprave the religious mind and cut it off from any Divine reality there may be? Who knows what distorted vision may have been passed down to us from those who have perpetrated such horrifying deeds? But, by the same token, given the vast ages that lie before us, who knows what enormous *improvements* future circumstances may slowly inspire in our spiritual genetic code?

The contrast between what may yet appear and the piddling few years of (deeply compromised) religion planet Earth has seen so far could hardly be more stark. It's easy for us to forget how ill-prepared our species may be for anything anywhere near ultimate insight, what with the flashy technologies that have led us to so dominate and alter the planet. Behind all the camouflage there is still an emotional crudity and a considerable propensity to violence. We are not so very different in these respects from the humans who first invented religion 50,000 years ago, whose violent tendencies are still inscribed in our genes. It is here, in this rather less than congenial environment, just a nanosecond ago in evolutionary terms, that religious ideas we today respectfully call "traditional" and "venerable" began to emerge. Perhaps we shouldn't be surprised—or regretful—at their passing. And perhaps, by the same token, we should begin to wonder what religious insights may arise if and when we manage to flush some of this immaturity out of our system, and go through the evolutionary changes that, say, another 100,000 or 1,000,000 years would bring.

Thus the blanket rejection of religion one often hears today from evolutionists is a non-sequitur, and indeed in serious tension with evolution's own animating ideas. But might an advocate of naturalism do better? Many will think that the amazing success of science provides enough of an argument for naturalistic belief, sufficient to justify it (and so to justify irreligious belief) even in a climate of evolutionary skepticism. Barbara Forrest, a philosopher at Southeastern Louisiana University whose view is typical in this connection, suggests that because of the continuing explanatory success of science, there is an "asymptotic decrease in the existential possibility of the supernatural to the point at which it is wholly negligible." And the other side of the coin, she suggests, is strong support for naturalism. Forrest puts it this way: naturalism is "a generalization of the cumulative results of scientific inquiry."

This argument faces certain difficulties, which the effects of temporal contextualization serve only to exacerbate. Suppose the apparent premise of Forrest's argument—that, over a long period, everything science has sought to explain has turned out to have a natural cause—is true. The conclusion of her generalization does not follow from it. It is too strong. Let's give her conclusion the weakest interpretation we can: *all events in nature have natural causes*. This may seem a small step for the argument to take, given the long period of success in assigning natural causes we have seen. But once temporally contextualized, we will say that the period of scientific success the Earth has witnessed so far is in fact incredibly short, and is so by science's own standards! The sample appealed to by the premise (everything science has sought to explain) is for this reason properly regarded as rather small and cannot be taken as representative of all events in nature—it is too small and too dubiously representative to support adequately Forrest's generalization, even on the weak interpretation we have given it. Of course there is an alternative conclusion. We might conclude from Forrest's premise that science will be successful in its *next* engagements with nature. This, in our evolutionary context, is a far more plausible inference, and also sufficient to motivate continuing scientific inquiry. But it is too weak to provide a jumping off point for the conclusion that all events in nature have natural causes.

And that's not the only problem to be found in the argument. It's important to notice that even if we agreed that all events in nature have natural causes, we still wouldn't have reached naturalism. The former claim doesn't add up to the claim that *all events whatever* have natural causes, nor does it entail it. It could be that all events in nature have natural causes and that there are non-natural events too, making naturalism false. And, in fact, even the claim *all events whatever have natural causes* wouldn't do the trick. For events could all have natural causes and yet have non-natural ones, too, if the latter were responsible for the operation of the former. Clearly it's a lot further from science to naturalism than the argument from the success of science allows.

At this point the defender of naturalism may switch gears, offering a different reason for believing her claim. The *methods* of religion, she may say, are entirely unimpressive by comparison with science's. This is a fairly common complaint. (Barbara Forrest mentions it, too.) Even if we take religion's methods to be ways of finding or doing very different things than are found or done in science, so it may be said, still there are problems. Suppose that, as is often claimed, experience of a Divine Ultimate and some sort of personal and social transformation are the goals of religion. Why, if there is anything to religion, are the means of achieving these goals not more effective? Religious people aren't obviously different from the non-religious in the qualities of character they display, for example. Indeed, the disanalogy here with science, whose methods are so effectively deployed, is quite striking, and should lead us to reject the supernatural and embrace naturalistic belief on methods-related grounds alone.

Suppose the premises used here are true. Even so, temporal contextualization will rightly make one hesitate to accept the argument. For why suppose that, were there anything to religion, religious methods of achieving religious goals as powerful as methods we see in science *would already have been developed*? Would we have been right to insist, in the Middle Ages, that what we saw then exhausted the potential of science? Various factors have contrived to keep religion at a much more primitive stage of development than science. Perhaps Colin McGinn could explain some of them. Certainly there are other factors reflecting human immaturity in the evaluative sense. But this state of affairs might well be rectified in the future. It could be, just for example, that with much time will come clearer and more universal and less conflicting instances of religious experience leading to clearer and more universal and more distinctive sorts of character development, which themselves lead to new and transformative forms of social organization. Thus any rejection of religion on methodological grounds is at best premature.

In a climate of evolutionary skepticism, therefore (a climate that science itself informs), naturalistic arguments are unable to deliver the goods. Naturalists regularly overestimate the accomplishments of science and underestimate the potential of religion. The success of science easily leads to a preoccupation with things that can be provided with natural causes. In our finite way, they have become "everything." Now, perhaps the natural world really *is* everything. Let me emphasize this thought lest my openness to it be missed. (It is important to remember that no critic of naturalistic belief who rests her argument on temporal contextualization will wish to say otherwise.) But equally, perhaps we are in a phase in which we are draining dry the scientific approach, seeing the world only from the peculiar slant our preoccupation affords. Perhaps there is much more to reality than will ever be dreamt of in science. If this idea causes distress for us as science-lovers, then the depth of our commitment to a no-holds-barred pursuit of understanding needs to be checked.

EVOLUTIONARY RELIGIOUS SKEPTICISM

So the old pessimism, based on naturalism, is premature. But that doesn't mean religious belief is in the clear. Nor is there any *alternative* way for irreligious belief to be justified. Let's think, now, about how the considerations of the last chapter can be applied to show this.

There is in fact a pretty straightforward case. Both religious and irreligious belief are rationally unsustainable and should be replaced, in diligent inquirers, by doubt. Why? Because they are inappropriate to our place in time. And why is that? Well, let's start with the six properties outlined near the end of the previous chapter and with religious belief. Religious beliefs, as the world has seen them in the past and knows them today, commonly exemplify *all six properties*, and often to a very high degree: they are precise, detailed, profound, attractive, ambitious, and controversial.

A precise claim has clear alternatives, which is to say that there are various ways in which it can be false. Take, for example, the claim that there is a personal God, as compared with the more vague notion that there is a transcendent reality of some kind. Being more precise, the first claim faces more alternatives—other and conflicting ways of carving up reality. A precise *and detailed* claim has more alternatives still: the claim that there is a personal God, given the many distinct omni-properties commonly assigned to the latter, is still an example. A precise, detailed, and *also profound* claim, one aiming at deep and comprehensive understanding—well, now you have more alternatives than could easily be counted. And you can bet that many of them are unnamed, and indeed could not be named—ever. Given their common implicit reference to ultimacy (here recall that the personal God's properties are *omni-*

properties: omnipotence, omniscience, and so on), we typically find in religious beliefs not just profundity but profundity in its most extreme form. Recognition of our place in time and the immaturity of our present condition should lead us to recognize that, in relation to such claims and their alternatives and the evidence pertaining to such things, we *might* just be stumbling around in the dark.

But now we graduate to the idea of a precise, detailed, and profound claim that is also attractive. Here neglect flourishes—just think of how often the attraction of their own "sense of religious reality" causes people to neglect the investigation of alternatives! And we are not yet at the end. For we have to accommodate McGinn by noticing that precise, detailed, profound, and attractive claims, when religious, are also hugely ambitious, in the sense that they reflect a sense of progress in regions that we know include matters very resistant to penetration by human intelligence. Think only of how the problems McGinn takes up in his *Problems in Philosophy* and declares insoluble—consciousness, self, meaning, and free will—may be child's play next to any ultimate reality *embracing* these more limited realities. If we aren't making headway with the former, why should we suppose ourselves able to make headway with the latter? (The concept of revelation won't help, and indeed precisely here the unjustified "sense of progress" mentioned above may be seen. For why suppose that we'd understand what we want revealed?) Finally, we come to controversy. Religious beliefs make precise, detailed, profound, attractive, and ambitious claims that are also, quite evidently, controversial. Due to our evaluative immaturity, the quality of religious investigations the world has already seen falls far short of what the true spirit of inquiry—a fierce and undiluted love of truth and understanding—would have produced, and nothing close to consensus in the present has been achieved. Controversy is about as deep and wide as can be imagined, with intellectuals found on all sides.

Such is the condition of religious belief. Should one hold such belief if temporally contextualized and on the side of truth and understanding? The question is rhetorical.

But the condition of irreligious belief (and thus of naturalism, which entails it) is hardly better. We've already seen that the route to a justification which appeals to naturalism is quite unpromising. We can, furthermore, point out that irreligious belief too is implicated in ambition and controversy, precision and profundity. Given its comprehensiveness, as construed here, we might describe it as directed to a big conjunction of propositions, with each conjunct except the last being the denial of some known religious belief, and the last conjunct being the claim that all unknown religious beliefs are false too. That would clearly mean it also possesses the property of detail! So irreligious belief displays at least five of our six properties. This makes it highly vulnerable to evolutionary skepticism, especially in the absence of a strong argument for naturalism, which might have provided countervailing support.

But the argument against irreligious belief I want to emphasize here is somewhat different, grounded more directly in what we saw in the last chapter to be our immaturity and its possible implications for our religious capacities. It is by the same token an independent path to the claim that *religious* belief is unjustified. This approach develops some suggestions about our capacities made in response to the old pessimism earlier in the chapter, and can also be seen as incorporating aspects of a McGinn-style ambition argument—all in a broader and deeper form of reasoning capable of standing on its own two feet.

We can start by noticing that precisely because of where we presently find ourselves, maturity-wise, in matters of religion, a great deal of intellectual progress on religious questions is still possible. It could be that because of our relative immaturity, religious notions and experiences of the past are entirely delusory, but on precisely the same grounds we should entertain the idea that they are just the first signs of much bigger and better things to come. Is the inchoate but overwhelming sense of the Divine that some report the "white noise" of an unfathomably great reality we haven't yet evolved the processing and filtering devices to handle, or pure fantasy? It would be premature to venture an opinion. (It is certainly hard to imagine Darwin believing anything on this one way or the other.) The ideas religious inquiry has turned up to this point may well be—borrowing from the eighteenth-century philosopher and skeptic David Hume—no more than the first rude essays of an infant species. Perhaps there will one day be knowledge of a Divine reality, but only when deeper capacities for commerce with the Divine have been developed.

However the "capacities" argument cuts both ways. Perhaps what deeper capacities will permit is the recognition that there is *no* Divine reality. We today are in no position to say how things would turn out, should inquiry long continue. It may be that many more rich layers of development and maturation, of very demanding sorts, requiring much time and cooperation between generations, will need to be laid down before any human being can reasonably hope to access such religious truths as there may be, or reasonably to rule out the existence of such truths. To think otherwise might be something like expecting the *Australopithecus afarensis* "Lucy" to be capable of understanding twentieth-century physics. So let the human species develop some of the more advanced capacities that may in the future come with a more advanced brain, or with the overcoming of violent tendencies, one wants to say, and think *then* about what the evidence supports concerning ultimate things!

On these grounds I propose that we are unjustified in believing that the human species or any of its members has *already developed* to the point where either the truth of some religious claim or the falsity of all religious claims (both actual and possible) could become available to our awareness. Such belief is just inappropriate to where we are in the temporal scheme of things. Of course we cannot say with any definiteness that the required development has not occurred, but we can't say it has either. There are simply too many glaring deficiencies in our relevant development so far and—given the depth and difficulty of matters involved—too many epistemically possible changes and intellectual enrichments in our future to make such a claim justified.

The religious skepticism based on our capacities that I am defending is a response to this awareness—quite an elementary awareness, though one seldom achieved. It is an attitude of doubt directed precisely to the proposition just mentioned—the proposition, to repeat, that the human species (or some member thereof) has already developed to the point where either the truth of some religious claim or the falsity of all religious claims can become available to our awareness. But it will be clear that following hard on the heels of this skepticism must be another: a skepticism directed to the view that some religious claim is *true* and, by the same token, to the view that *no* religious claim is true. Our immaturity (in the combined sense) is fatal to justified belief of either proposition.

A variation on the capacities argument emphasizes possible future religious abilities rather than our inabilities, and begins with this question: What do you suppose we might be able to come up with in the way of new religious ideas given another million years? In her book of the same name, Karen Armstrong speaks of "the great transformation" in religious consciousness that occurred during the

Axial Age, mentioned earlier. The Axial Age, she says, was a time of "spiritual genius," producing some of the best thinkers and thoughts of Taoism, Confucianism, Buddhism, among other traditions. Suppose this is true. How many more "axial ages" may yet lie ahead? (A synchronic conception of religion obscures this thought from us, but a more appropriate diachronic one will bring it into view.) Might they produce a detailed and convincing perspective entailing the existence of a Divine reality but one quite at odds with any detailed picture of the Divine available today? Who can say? Much is epistemically possible here, and clearly we are in no position to judge that all the important results are in. What we can say is that if results of this sort, properly believed to be true, *were* to be achieved in future, irreligious belief and also all detailed religious beliefs dating to the present would then have to be given up. *But if so then these beliefs have to be given up now.* For if it is epistemically possible that a view I now hold will turn out to be false in the deep future, then (by the definition of epistemic possibility) I have no good reason to believe it will *not* turn out to be false—which is to say that I have no good reason now to believe it true.

If we really are interested in the inquirer's goals of truth and understanding, such considerations must represent an important wake-up call, and revive us from the complacency of religious or irreligious belief. But perhaps we're not quite awake yet. So let's try the evolutionary argument for religious skepticism once again, in a somewhat different way.

I have been emphasizing our immaturity—this new and previously unacknowledged factor supporting skepticism. The last way of developing such reasoning I will offer combines this point in a new way with one that has been lurking in the background and occasionally making a more conspicuous appearance—as when we mentioned McGinn. This reticent point, in a variety of shades, has been emphasized before by religious skeptics: human *limitations* in quest of the *unlimited*.

Now, you might think that the two notions I have mentioned, limitation and immaturity, are in one way or another conceptually linked. But when speaking here of our limitations I have in mind something one may readily acknowledge about finite beings like us even without being temporally contextualized. The basic idea is captured by the "mitigated" skepticism of David Hume, who continually reminds his readers of the cognitive constraints under which we labor and our proneness to cognitive errors, instructing us to limit our thinking to the matters that "are best adapted to the narrow limits of human understanding." Those limits seemed to him, and have seemed to many others, to fall well *this* side of facts about the ultimate nature or destiny of things, which religious belief of course purports to reach.

So we have from the skeptical tradition—and developed with an evolutionary twist by McGinn—this familiar point: human beings, as finite creatures, are deeply limited beings; and our limitations may severely hamper our pursuit of knowledge about ultimate things. (It is certainly a point whose force was felt by Darwin.) But there is also an unfamiliar move, now made possible because we've learned about our immaturity in deep time, which in combination with the other will permit us to increase its power many times over. For we can reason as follows. Surely the very least to be concluded from our *limitations* is that a long process of very high-quality religious inquiry would be required to justify religious or irreligious belief. And surely the very least we can conclude from our *immaturity* is that we have not yet engaged in such inquiry. Thus, even more obviously than before, religious and irreligious belief are shown to be inappropriate and intellectually unjustified for beings such as we are.

* * *

Looking back at religion past, religious people tend to see venerable wisdom and revelatory insight, while the irreligious see horrors and misbegotten ideas. In concluding this book's second pair of chapters, I want to point out how each side would think differently about religion, were the future turn recommended in the first pair to be made successfully. Indeed, their lines of vision would converge.

What the religious would see is that it is only our non-temporalized perspective that makes us think of great age and venerability in connection with the traditions, and that our best religious ideas and most revealing religious experiences may well lie ahead of us. What the irreligious would see is that it may only be human immaturity that is manifested in the horrors and misbegotten ideas of much past religion, and only our non-temporalized perspective that makes us think that if there *were* something to religion, it would have been revealed by now. Having thus had their vision expanded, both the religious and the irreligious would be converted by evolutionary considerations to religious doubt or skepticism—the one side from belief, the other from disbelief.

The essential point in all of this is that we are much closer to the beginning of a proper assessment of religious possibilities than we may care to admit. The need for an evolutionary religious skepticism stares us in the face when we consider this point with due care and the inquirer's gaze—a gaze that values genuine understanding much more than any short-term imposter.

5

The New Optimism

I said to my soul, be still and wait without hope
For hope would be hope for the wrong thing; wait without
   love
For love would be love of the wrong thing; there is yet faith
But the faith and love and the hope are all in the waiting.
Wait without thought, for you are not ready for thought:
So the darkness shall be the light, and the stillness the
   dancing.

T. S. Eliot, Four Quartets

In the statement that accompanies his portrait in Steve Pyke's gallery of philosophers, Timothy Williamson, the current Wykeham Professor of Logic at Oxford, links logic to good poetry, finding in both "a precise and radical imagination." Darwin also appreciated poetry—though the most famous expression of this appreciation was somewhat rueful and past-tinged. Late in life, after all his great works were behind him, Darwin remarked in his autobiography that if he had it to do all over again, he would read some poetry at least once a week. Neglecting the "higher aesthetic tastes," said he, could well be the source of a variety of problems. It might even be "injurious to the intellect."

If the help that poetry can provide to the intellect is to be inferred from Williamson's comment, then, at least where science is concerned, Darwin needn't have worried. For he had imagination in spades, and his was certainly an imagination both radical and precise. Unfortunately, it would be a mistake to speak in similar terms about what humans have come up with on the relations between broadly Darwinian ideas and religion. Here, a lack of imagination has prevented us from reaching some important realizations.

The first one, central to the half of this book just completed, may be experienced as radically deflationary by the religious: it suggests a new way, unnoticed even by traditional religion's evolutionary critics, of showing that religious belief is rationally unsustainable for twenty-first-century members of *H. sapiens*. According to this critique, religious belief is just inappropriate to where we're located temporally. But again we have only one side of the story. The other side is about how a brand new way of being religious emerges and may find the needed support when we become temporally contextualized, a religiousness that not only tolerates but thrives on skepticism. Thus, if before we were feeling a new pessimism, after the remaining chapters there may be a strange new optimism!

Perhaps it takes a radical imagination to move comfortably among such subjects. However that may be, in this second half of the book my question is how our imaginings about such things can be made more precise. As we enter this new discussion, let's try, in good Darwinian fashion, to hold prejudgment at bay, considering, in ways that even the Catholic T. S. Eliot might not have countenanced, how stillness could be dancing, and darkness light.

RELIGION FOR PRIMITIVES

A long skinny balloon is being inflated and slowly expanding ever further away from a starting point (don't worry, I won't let it pop). As the plastic is stretched you can clearly distinguish parts of the balloon. When it's fully inflated, you mark these off from each other with a felt-tip pen: here's the first couple of inches; here's the second, and so on. Before it was inflated you could not make these distinctions or look at these parts of the balloon separately, but now you can.

Similarly, when we achieve the long view afforded by awareness of the deep future, we get a stretched conception of our time, seeing also the many that will come after it: here's the first couple hundred thousand years; here's the second, and so on. We think of reflective intelligence on our planet getting well started perhaps 50,000 years ago and continuing through the present and—we hope—into the nearer bit of the deep future, thinking of this stretch of time *separately* from the others. Of course the dividing lines between our time and others will to some extent be arbitrarily placed. But even if we do think of our time as enduring for as long as 200,000 years, we see that it is only the first of many—as many as 5,000!—in which reflective intelligence may be found.

One of my central claims is that we have to be able to go through this process and get that first moment, that first stage of reflective intelligence, squarely before our minds, considering it *separately* from the others that will follow, if we're going to think adequately about the role religion might have in our culture and assess accurately its possible contributions to cultural evolution. One way of considering this discussion is in terms of what philosophers call a debate between faith and reason. Reason—understood broadly as whatever in us incites or serves a love of truth and understanding—has, as we've seen, been getting way ahead of itself in forming views, yea or nay, on the epistemic worth of religious ideas. A love of truth and under-standing *well* served will show just this. But some of the old questions can still be asked. Must faith be odious to reason? Is there any form of religion that reason instead can tolerate or even commend? Only now such questions will receive a temporal inflection and be broadened a bit to permit a wider cultural involvement in the discussion. For example: Is such-and-such a religiousness—perhaps one commonly exemplified among us—just wrong for reflective but primitive crea-tures like us? Is it inappropriate given our early stage of development? But also: might there be a new form of religiousness that *is* appropri-ate to our time?

In the absence of a temporalist perspective we haven't been in a position to consider things in this way, just as before the balloon is inflated one can't consider the various parts contributing to its elongation or their specific features and how they differ. Instead, just like everyone coming before us, we have tended to think of the present time simply as "now." Sometimes the past is taken in with the present and "now" is also taken as "the end." This is all very mislead-ing. And it has also misled us in our thinking about the place of religion in our culture. In particular, it has prevented the concept of evolutionary religion from being formed. This is the notion, just mentioned, of a form of religion appropriate to or befitting intelli-gence at a first stage of evolutionary development: religion for primi-tives who hope to evolve into something more, religion that might *promote* such positive cultural evolution. This would be a form of religion we regard as desirable or admirable precisely given how things are now (desirable, let's say, if, given how things are now, such religious practice contributes to our flourishing and so is good *for* us; admirable, if it is to be viewed as good whether or not good for us, perhaps because deserving of respect or some such thing). Clearly the balloon has to be inflated, allowing us to see that first stage of reflective intelligence and its distinctive features clearly, before we can even begin to think about such a thing as evolutionary religion.

If there is a form of religion appropriate to our time—an evolutionary religiousness able to make a case for itself—then we will have a solution for the cultural problems in which religion is caught, including the so-called problem of faith and reason. After all, properly temporalized we will also see that we don't need to solve this problem for all times, only for our own. In the next chapter I will offer a proposal including a fairly precise description of how I think religion might best be conceived in order to achieve the "evolutionary" status just described. In the present chapter my wish is simply to suggest some general parameters for this investigation. Naturally I will seek to develop these ideas as strongly as I can and to bring out their attractive features. But they are proposals, and it may be that parts of them will need to be refined or dropped. My main aim is to get us started in the development of a temporalist perspective on religion.

One thing these proposals indicate, if it wasn't obvious already, is that what comes with this new evolutionary solution to religion's problems is going to be a new way of being religious. Indeed, we are thinking quite deliberately about how to evolve a new form of religion—this of course is another reason for calling it *evolutionary* religion. Someone offering our solution can therefore appear to be trying to get such a new way of being religious established—to get it going out there in the big wide world. I have no such pretensions. (This of course is compatible with thinking that some new form of religiousness is worthy of being realized.) Even if temporalism about religion is on the right track, and indeed even if everything I say in this and subsequent chapters about evolutionary religion is correct, it might only be in some later generation, after deep time is more fully internalized, that such a new form of religion takes hold (notice that given a stretched conception of where we are temporally, such a future moment might still belong to our time). Or it may never take hold at all. A lot depends on the sort of discussion we have with each other, and to this I *do* want to contribute.

Against that background, let me set out the general parameters. What I have in mind here are *necessary conditions* of evolutionary religion—general features that anything properly so-called would possess—which we can use in any subsequent attempt to track down our quarry. Evolutionary religion, so I say, will be

(1) **diachronic instead of synchronic,** sensitive not only to what's happening in the present but to processes and changes unfolding over vast periods of time taking us from the past far into the future, and willing to reinterpret religious attitudes and ideas for our own time accordingly (religious diachronism);

(2) **cognitively modest** on account of what can be learned about natural selection operating in the past as well as the Great Disparity, expressing religious intellectual commitment in a manner compatible with nonbelief or skepticism about the most profound and controversial matters, including even religious ones (religious skepticism);

(3) **forward looking and patient,** concerned for the development of *greater* religious maturity and insight rather than preoccupied with the past and depending on the authority of founder figures (religious developmentalism); and

(4) **attentive to the evolutionary benefits of redesigned religion,** thinking about how religion itself might help us evolve toward ever greater maturity in all areas of human life, in particular functioning as part of the solution to our evaluative immaturity instead of part of the problem (religious pragmatism).

These conditions are intimately related to one another. Indeed, the first might be thought to enfold the rest, since the other conditions I'll be emphasizing can be seen as ways of being true to that one. But each is also distinct in certain ways requiring that it be considered in its own right. Let's now look at each more closely.

RELIGIOUS DIACHRONISM

Evolutionary religion will allow us to be farsighted in every way—and also in the dimension of time. This is a rather basic part of the reason for calling it *evolutionary*. It sees various aspects of our experience—including religion—as propensities having many possible realizations, as features of human life and perhaps other forms of life to come that can in important ways grow and change through-out the lives of intelligent species and of the planet. It sees that it would be absurd to ignore all this when thinking about what religion in our own time ought to look like.

What this means is that evolutionary religion will be sensitive to both past and future. It's important to notice that although different in some fundamental ways from traditional religion, it need not simply reject the past. Rather, temporally contextualized, this form of religion will be able to look both forward and back. For example, stirring expressions of human frailty and religious longing in many existing religious scriptures, or the psychological insights included in the Four Noble Truths and Eight-fold Path of the Buddha, may continue to edify and inspire. And when it comes to the *ideas* that will be central, evolutionary religion will not give up the transcendent reference—inconsistent with metaphysical naturalism—that other forms of religiousness have carried with them through millennia past. Indeed, it will see its willingness to modify elsewhere (see: religious skepticism), along with temporalist arguments of the sort we've already developed against naturalistic belief, as affording a unique rationale for persisting with a non-naturalistic picture of the world. At the same time a sensitivity also to the future will lead evolutionary religion to give *minimal content* to the central object of religious intellectual concern.

In religion as we've had it so far, one instead finds many propos-itional details. Think, for example, of orthodox Christian doctrine concerning the existence of a personal and triune God who created the world and also lived and died in it as a man in order to facilitate, for humans, the life of the Kingdom of God. Or take the Hindu idea that through awareness of reality as one and spiritual, our souls, eternal but bound by the law of karma to the world of matter, may be released from the cycle of rebirth and realize identity with the One Reality, Brahman. Rather a lot of details here! And my present point is just that such details can easily militate against future development if made the central object of religious intellectual commitment. How so? By preventing openminded and openhearted exploration of detailed conceptions at odds with them.

The point is that if we are to think of ourselves as being at a very early stage of religious development, then we need to be as open as possible to *very many* possible formulations of religious ideas—in-cluding many that haven't occurred to anyone yet. And we will need to consider how our behavior in the present may make such vital discoveries of the future, should they be waiting for us, more or less likely. Having done so we will see, I think, that it would be counterproductive to become *committed* to any particular detailed formulation, whether believingly or in some other way (more on the variety of attitudinal options here in a moment). Now, perhaps it will seem that such a commitment need not prevent proper investigation of alternative views so long as a love of truth is also present in the one so committed. Perhaps it *need* not. But human nature and human primitivity being what they are, it very often may do so, and so there is reason for anyone offering evolutionary religion as a *new* option to the religious marketplace to seek an alternative stance. Indeed, investigation of many different actual and possible religious details, without commitment to any of them, might beneficially be made *part* of religious practice for beings as immature as we are, and woven into evolutionary religion wherever it is found. But this doesn't mean that nothing at all can serve as an appropriate center for the intellectual life of religion. We simply need to start thinking more generally than we are accustomed to doing—looking for a broad framework proposition that can help us organize and unify many diverse religious activities. We need something set at a good distance from us, conceptually speaking: not so distant as to be incapable of touching us, but not so close and defined in its features as to obscure the many alternatives lined up behind it and make us forget our place in time.

Perhaps in the distant future we will be able to afford the luxury of having individuals and groups live by the detailed *versions* of some central religious idea that, after all the preceding investigation, seem most probable and inviting to them, but for the forseeable future, any such indulgence must, I suggest, only stand in the way of the complete shift of orientation required to make deep human progress in matters religious more likely. It would threaten to slow any progress toward religious enlightenment that may be possible for us. (Of course if we're looking for what's most probable, we'll have reason to plump for a general idea over any of its detailed versions anyway.)

The other side of the coin, it's good to see, is a new optimism as to the ability of Earthly creatures at some point properly to make those epistemic judgments yea or nay that are now proscribed. This has now become imaginable. And, as we've noticed, there is no more reason to suppose that what we'll discover is the *falsehood* of basic religious ideas than to suppose that their truth will be confirmed. A temporalist perspective can for this reason be intellectually and spiritually liberating. Religion here gets a big new lease on life.

It's important to realize that we're talking about *robust* religion— religion that continues to hold before itself the idea of explicit inter- action with a transcendent Divine reality of the sort that certain reductionist accounts of religion, eager to conform themselves to the regnant naturalistic impulse by restricting religious concerns to moral matters and the like, have already given up. There is no need for religion to give up on this. Everyone surely will agree that if religion *could* deliver, the result would be important, amazing, won- derful...And the temporalist orientation pushes us to be at least open to the idea of humanity over much time evolving toward just such a state. Indeed, it entertains the thought that Earthly intelli- gence may discover things far deeper and more wonderful than humans have yet developed the capacities to appreciate. Thus such an orientation is not nearly as corrosive, religiously, as it might at first appear to be.

In the next chapter I will provide more detail about the notion of a religious intellectual center free of detail—a specific way of realizing such a thing. For now let's move on to the issue of how a practitioner of evolutionary religion will *relate* herself, mentally, to any such idea.

RELIGIOUS SKEPTICISM

The basic answer is that she will find a way of relating herself to it compatible with evolutionary skepticism. Though skepticism is sometimes linked with cynicism or excessive negativity, all the term *means*, at least for us (and we've seen this to be the dominant understanding in philosophy), is doubt or uncertainty, being in a state involving neither belief nor disbelief in relation to whatever claim is at issue. And although the point is often missed, such a state it is possible to combine with something much more affirmative and positive: despite doubt there may, for example, grow an intention to act as would be appropriate if the proposition in question were true. Acting on such an intention despite doubt is more commonly done, and the reasons for doing so more plentiful and various, than many of us realize. It may be required for *survival* in some cases. If you're stranded on an isolated island in the Pacific you may not be able to believe that you'll be discovered, but you'd better act as though that is the case!

Here careful readers will notice an allusion to the concept of belief-less acceptance introduced a couple of chapters back. What someone inclined to defend naturalism may now suggest is that this is a notion to which would-be naturalists convinced by my skepticism, as much as anyone else, may help themselves. Indeed—I agree. But, imbued with reason's love of truth and understanding, we will be required to look for criteria by which to determine, for this large-scale view or that, whether it should under present circumstances be positively greeted, mentally, or not. And it's not at all obvious that naturalism must come out ahead when they are applied. (There will be more on this in the book's last chapter.) Certainly, a reconfigured religious perspective may now hope for as full a hearing as any other. The rules have changed. Indeed, we've got a new game.

It's important to recognize that because the game has changed—because we've become temporally reoriented—the attitude we find to substitute for religious belief will not be some unhappy fall-back option or "second best." It may occur to us that the *beginning* of religion pretty obviously *should* be cognitively modest, given the multi-level maturity that a real grasp of basic facts concerning the Divine might presuppose. Belief tells us that we've arrived at the end of the investigative road. We should rather think of ourselves as just setting out, as humans, on the journey of inquiry. The tendency of religion in past and present to underwrite an attitude of confident believing is not an essential feature of religiousness but rather a stage-related *error* we can weed out with temporal contextualization. (This is of course consistent with religious belief being appropriate to some future stage of religion.) And we should be happy to have it gone so that we are freed to pursue religion in a more appropriate manner—perhaps one that will lead in time to beliefs having a much greater likelihood of being true.

We need a more sensitive power of discrimination where human attitudes toward such claims as the claim that there is an ultimate Divine reality are concerned. And here philosophy can be of help. Philosophers call attitudes of the sort in question "propositional attitudes." Naming whatever claim or proposition may be in question "p," it's easy to see that you could *fear* that p; be *angry* that p; *hope* that p; *desire* that p; and, yes, also *believe* that p. Some of these attitudes clearly are positive, and others are not. And there are attitudes that are positive about a proposition in a manner analogous to what we see in the case of belief that p, though without *entailing* such belief. The attitude of accepting that p is of course one, but there are others too.

We might, for example, distinguish between believing that p and believing that p is probable on the available evidence. The latter belief, though in a sense positive about p, falls short of simple belief that p, and this may be viewed as a good thing by anyone aware at some level of the problem of Total Evidence. One could be in doubt about p, in the relevant sense of neither believing nor disbelieving it, while nonetheless holding this more qualified belief about the quality of the available evidential support for p. Variations on the theme quickly suggest themselves, such as the state of believing that p is more probable on the available evidence than any alternative to p known to us. This option is emphasized by the Oxford philosopher Richard Swinburne in his influential book *Faith and Reason*. It is also possible belieflessly to *assume* that p or *trust* that p. (Probablilistic beliefs of the sort previously mentioned may or may not play a role in such attitudes.) The latter idea of beliefless trust is developed and defended by Robert Audi, a philosopher at Notre Dame University; the former of beliefless assumption by philosopher Daniel Howard-Snyder of Western Washington University. And this does not exhaust the list. The point is that when the grip of the concept of *believing* on our way of thinking about religious intellectual attitudes is broken, alternatives readily present themselves.

Let's return for a bit to acceptance. The state of accepting a proposition L. Jonathan Cohen, long at Queen's College, Oxford, defines as follows: "To accept that p is to have or adopt a policy of deeming, positing, or postulating that p—i.e., of including that proposition or rule among one's premises for deciding what to do or think in a particular context, whether or not one feels it to be true that p." For Cohen, to believe that p is, by contrast, to be disposed to *feel it to be true* that p. Belief is thus involuntary, involving a feeling or sense, whereas acceptance is voluntary. And thus even where one is involuntarily in doubt about p, neither believing nor disbelieving it, one can still graft onto one's doubt, as it were, a state of acceptance.

Acceptance, as noted earlier, is often called for even when belief is rationally and perhaps also psychologically impossible. And it is differently related to evidence. Rational belief requires good evidence of truth, but alternative attitudes like acceptance, because compatible with being in doubt, don't always do so—even while requiring their own rather different form of support. Here we are typically at a point *before* evidence sufficient for straightforward belief that p is available. These attitudes are indeed ones for which good evidence is the wrong kind of support. If we had good evidence, we wouldn't need them! Other kinds of support are relevant instead—usually broadly pragmatic ones. Perhaps acceptance is in some context required by one's moral commitments (you accept that your partner has not betrayed you though the evidence is mounting up) or by one's legal obligations (you accept that the defendant is innocent since you're on a jury in his trial even though he sure looks guilty—this example is Cohen's), or perhaps it's needed to achieve some important personal goal or a goal held in common with others (you're still trying to find a lost toddler after weeks of fruitless searching and accept that success is not out of reach). Here there may be little support for belief—indeed, you may be unable to believe—and yet there is something positive, mentally, that you can do and perhaps should do in relation to the proposition at issue.

Coming back to religion and evolution, there is no reason why these results might not be appropriated religiously, in the evolution of a nonbelieving attitude of *faith* appropriate to our time. In some quarters, this is already happening. Thus we have William Alston, long at Syracuse University in New York, and a leading epistemologist of the late twentieth century, developing a beliefless conception of religious faith by reference to Cohen's work on acceptance. And other prominent figures are arguing similarly. In the next chapter, I will outline my own favored alternative. This work in recent philosophy of religion hasn't yet caught on in a big way, but that, I would argue, is because most of us are still standing by Darwin's Door looking *back*. When temporal contextualization takes hold, everything could change.

If religiously authentic and rational alternatives to believing compatible with doubt and weak evidence do become available, we will have a deeply important cultural result. For we will disqualify, at a stroke, the most common criticisms of religion, which all presuppose that faith is belief-based. The criticism of belief has for centuries nurtured the sense that religion is in serious trouble, because evidence sufficient for reasonable belief seems not to be available. At first, evolutionary religious skepticism seems only to add force to this criticism. But a properly formulated criticism of this sort would add an all-important qualification: religion is in serious trouble *so long as it continues to base itself on belief*. And why must it do so? Evolutionary religion, if indeed it is *evolutionary* religion, should call us to embrace the loss of belief as a possible step to the rebirth of religion in a nonbelieving form more appropriate to our time and to the claims of reason.

RELIGIOUS DEVELOPMENTALISM

Nicholas Wade, at the end of his recent book *The Faith Instinct*, talks about how religion "needs to undergo a second transformation, similar in scope to the transition from hunter gatherer religion to that of settled societies," with the result being one in which, among other things, religion has found "a way to be equally true to emotion and to reason." And the well known journalist John Horgan, in an online discussion with journalist and author Robert Wright, sponsored by the Firedoglake Book Salon, had this to say in closing: "I also hope, and expect, because we're already headed in this direction, that more and more people will abandon traditional religions and seek out and create forms of spirituality that don't carry so much baggage with them." Wright, for his own part, at the end of his recent book *The Evolution of God*, says that "there's room" and indeed "an urgent need" for "more progress" in religion. "Is it crazy," he asks, "to imagine a day when the Abrahamic faiths renounce . . . the claim to specialness of the whole Abrahamic enterprise? . . . . Changes this radical have already happened, again and again. Another transformation would be nothing new." Though his book is mostly about the past evolution of religious thought and practice in the theistic traditions of the west, Wright—precisely *because* of the important religious changes he finds in the past—is open to future evolution: his book's last line suggests that "how far humanity has traveled along the path of spiritual evolution" is an open question.

When talking about religion or spirituality, all of these writers evidently are to some extent thinking *developmentally* in the sense relevant to our third condition of evolutionary religion. (Spirituality, I will assume, is just religion in the neglected personal sense: religiousness.) And many religious people and spiritual seekers today are at least implicitly doing the same. But references to a fully developmental view of religion in contemporary literature are themselves undeveloped—hints, allusions, suggestions only. Evolutionists have, of course, had a lot to say about religion as it existed in the near and distant past, but perhaps because of the peculiarly scientific interests that can keep them peering backward in time, they are more inclined to think of present-day stirrings in religion as restricted to some final stage of such past developments than as potentially marking a first stage of future ones.

Things didn't need to be this way. In any case, evolutionary religion will enshrine a fully developmental perspective, thinking of Earthly creatures as just getting started on the path toward religious insight and maturity but potentially able to make it all the way there, and thinking of ourselves as needing to do the things that will make arrival at that destination more likely. This is just the opposite of the usual religious approach, which involves looking back in time to the authoritative pronouncements or example of founder figures—people like Jesus of Nazareth or Siddhartha Gautama (the Buddha). There is of course nothing to prevent us, in evolutionary religion, from taking seriously what was said or done by people like Jesus or the Buddha. Indeed, certain goals of religious practice, such as personal transformation in the direction of deeper maturity, may in some way be bound up with their example. We may even think that certain of their ideas and practices are ones we want to build on in seeking to bring humanity closer to those goals. But none of this implies that we have to think of such individuals as having fully reached those goals themselves or as uniquely able to tell us how to do so.

For readers still wondering why we should be thus patient in spiritual matters—future-minded instead of resting on past authority—here are a few additional points. First, religion is, to say the very least, extremely ambitious. When talking about religious ideas we include the most difficult and profound matters to have been entertained by human minds. Indeed, it's natural to associate religion with a quest for the *ultimate* in reality and goodness. And we wisely allow more time for making progress with the most difficult matters—perhaps ones far transcending in difficulty and ambition the puzzles of philosophy that led McGinn into pessimism—than for others. A second point is that if religion is right, then what it concerns is not only ultimate in the metaphysical sense but also of ultimate importance. Other things being equal, it's wise to give extra time to the exploration of matters that, if capable of yielding truths at all, will yield truths mattering that much. Third, evolution—whether biological or cultural—is often slow. Take this point as enhancing each of the other two. If evolution is slow, then we *certainly* shouldn't expect to have got very far thinking about ultimate things in a few thousand years. And if the results are of ultimate importance, then we *certainly* shouldn't give up yet.

Remember that this third point is well grounded in science. Indeed, Darwin, the hero of evolutionary critics of religion such as Richard Dawkins, rested on it much of his case for a new picture of nature. Darwin's was an important "what if?" question about the past. What if all the glories of nature we see around us are the result of very small changes accumulating over an incredibly long time under the influence of natural selection? Most of us have yet to embrace an equally compelling what-if about our future: what if many other small changes in the intellectual, social, moral, emotional dimensions of life over an incredibly long time, guided by the restlessly curious human mind (or by the intelligence of species following us), will immeasurably enhance the glories of intellectual achievement on our planet, leading also to a much richer and deeper picture of ultimate things? Given everything we've seen so far in this book, can the evolutionarily minded rule out such a possibility, rationally forming beliefs incompatible with it? I think it's clear that the answer is no. To do otherwise is simply to fail to summon the "effort of the imagination to escape from the prison of familiar timescale" that (as noted in Chapter 1) Dawkins rightly recommends to us.

RELIGIOUS PRAGMATISM

An important aspect of anything deserving the label "evolutionary religion" and developed within a temporalist frame of reference will be attention to the evolutionary *benefits* of redesigned religion within the wider culture. Here we are thinking about how religion of a certain sort might help us evolve toward greater maturity in various departments of human life, thus being itself an important moment of cultural evolution, part of the solution to the complex and interwoven ills of human life at our primitive stage of development instead of part of the problem.

Recently there has been much discussion about how very bad religion has been, humanly speaking—how so often it has stood in the way of the advancement of important human goals, whether individual or societal. Writers influenced by evolutionary thought, such as Christopher Hitchens, have been writing books with titles like Hitchens' own: *God is Not Great: How Religion Poisons Everything.* (That the sub-title cannot help but overstate the problem is indicated by the title, which restricts our attention to god-oriented religion.) Hitchens focuses somewhat one-sidedly on all the terrible things for which theistic religion is responsible, forgetting or ignoring much of the good. Naturally, this has been pointed out to him (and to the many others arguing similarly) by a cadre of theists, who are writing books with titles like Keith Ward's *Is Religion Dangerous?* It was also pointed out by the former British prime minister, Tony Blair, who took up the cudgels for religion (read: theistic religion) in a debate with Hitchens before a packed Roy Thomson Hall in Toronto. Such games of religious 'tis and 'tisn't seem virtually always to be going on.

What hasn't been observed in all this is that the popular games are focused entirely on traditional religion—familiar religion of the past—and usually quite parochially on traditional theistic religion at that. A discerning evolutionist will surely want to look past all the short-sighted and one-sided talk about religion and point us to the future, when religion may grow up and, in so doing, help all the rest of us to grow up, too. Functioning not as biologists or journalists or philosophers but as human beings, evolutionists should certainly be prompted to notice how great a force religion might be for good— for evolution *beyond* the very same human deficiencies in which religion has so often been implicated—if once it could appropriately be redirected.

Shortly after writing those words, I acquired a copy of Christian de Duve's latest book—*Genetics of Original Sin: The Impact of Natural Selection on the Future of Humanity.* In it he argues that natural selection's short-term interests have made humanity's problems, which will require widescale and concerted efforts directed toward long-term goods, all the more difficult. He also emphasizes how religion might be of great help here, if it could be enlisted on the side of the future. E. O. Wilson has made a similar point in *The Creation: An Appeal to Save Life on Earth.* Both writers, however, are focused on Christianity. And Christianity has tended to be much more concerned with moral minutiae than with lofty themes such as saving the environment. Many conservative Christians, as we have seen, have trouble accepting even the evolutionary past, so how much success will appeals to the future grounded in evolutionary thought have in reaching them?

Stirrings of more helpful efforts among Christians can be seen in the work of certain revisionist or reductionist approaches to religion, which would have us focus our attention purely on moral ideas. They are exemplified by Gretta Vospers, minister in the United Church of Canada and author of the recent book *With or Without God*, who reduces religious language and the life of the religious community pretty much entirely to the provoking and sustaining of constructive social action. The problem is that religion, to keep its hold on us, and to gain a new hold on those who are now its cultured despisers or just apathetic, needs to appeal to both heart *and* mind; as we heard Nicholas Wade say, it needs to be "equally true to emotion *and* to reason." But the revisions and reductions on offer sunder this conjunction. Any straightforward move to push a purely ethical "religion" shorn of all robust references to the transcendent is likely to end up with something lacking also the peculiar and haunting depths of emotional power that traditional religion at its best represents.

Evolutionary religion offers us a way around these dilemmas. By being intellectually minimalist but skeptical and imaginative in equal measure, and by keeping the idea of a Divine reality, though out of respect for its content and our primitivity keeping it at something of a distance, temporally—in these ways, evolutionary religion can provide a framework for a reboot, religiously, that holds on to what will move us and sets aside what will prevent us from being moved in the right direction. As we've seen, a diachronic conception of religion permits us to consider that religion might appropriately be very different at an earlier time in the history of humanity than at conceivable later ones. Now we can add that the goals of religion today might indeed in some way be bound up with helping the species *reach* later times.

Any genuinely evolutionary form of religion, tempered by temporal contextualization, will start from a recognition of our immaturity—intellectually, morally, and in other ways. And it will build the overcoming of such immaturities into religious practice, finally allowing religion to make good on all its promises about humility, which in the world as it is are regularly trumped by the arrogance of detailed religious believing loudly defended. With the heightened and enriched emotion it would permit and the social cohesion it would promote, such religion, were it ever to be realized widely, would provide a framework for realizing ideals held in common by the greatest religious and secular saints of the past. It would be a powerful force for positive cultural evolution.

GENNA'S IDEA

To help the points I've made in this chapter find their way home, and to prepare us for the next chapter, I close with a story. This story is about happenings in a possible world somewhat different from the actual. In this world there is a planet very like our Earth and a species similar to the human, but it is a species whose early period of development diverges from our own in certain important respects. Our counterpart species on this planet emerges from the evolutionary muck quite preoccupied with what is close at hand, with a hard-won ability to distinguish between appearance and reality in that domain, on which ability its continued survival indeed depends. The members of this species are no-nonsense individuals who, as we begin our story, are negotiating their way through the ever-present challenges of a precarious existence, enjoying its occasional pleasures and closely bound one to another in stable communities, but not often pausing to lift their eyes to the stars. Not yet.

But then one of their number (let's call her Genna) has a profound new experience. Unable to sleep and standing outside her tent flap, gazing at a spider's web, she suddenly has a sense of possibilities greater than ever seen or imagined, a prolonged and astonishingly rich experience in which she seems plunged into something that comes to her from every direction and yet from none, further away than the mountains hunched over the valley and yet closer than her own breath and quivering with the spider on its web. Something that fills everything with a light at once inviting and frightening. Something that with its terror and with its joy breaks up all of the categories by which she had perceived the world into kindling for the fire and yet leaves her feeling utterly complete and whole.

The experience endures for some time and then slowly the normal appearances reassert themselves. The spider still hangs at the center of its web, twirling in the wind. Naturally shaken by the experience, Genna is quite unsure what to make of it as she goes about her physical tasks the next day. Belonging, as she does, to a sensible species, she is not convinced that she has been introduced to a new feature of reality; she is not awash in conviction, rushing about seeking to generate the same in others. Moreover, she is reminded by hard events that life in the world of day does not exactly match the wonders of the night: there is struggle and accident and illness and death before the sun has once more circled the sky, and it is easy to be again preoccupied with what is close at hand, with what can be seen and touched and tasted; easy to be led by the often *bitter* taste of life to doubt that there really is a deeper reality that is the deepest and most frighteningly beautiful of all things.

Nevertheless the thought of such a reality lingers, insinuating itself into the cracks between moments of physical activity. Genna finds herself wondering what else she might discern if what she apparently experienced were real and if, freed from the contradictions of her experience, she were able to detect more of the details of its nature. But none of the particular conceptions she is able to spin from her imagination is satisfying. None—not even the idea of a great and powerful but invisible *person* that comes to mind one day while caring for an ill child and remembering her once capable husband—measures up to the reality encountered outside her tent. The best she can do is to push her thinking in the opposite direction: to take facets of her everyday experience, extend them as far as possible, and then imagine something beyond even that. So when swimming to the bottom of a tidal pool she imagines a tidal pool with no bottom; when gazing at the sheltering mountains she imagines a mountain that remains perpetually on the horizon, no matter how far she walks; when she feels the sun, she imagines a light that can illuminate even the darkest night and warm her even on the coldest days.

Though not believing that what her imaginings contain is real (she belongs to a sensible species, after all), Genna finds that holding the idea of a reality deeper and greater and more radically but positively transformative than any other before her mind makes of each day a better and brighter—and somehow a *bigger*—thing. Sometimes, though not always as powerfully as before, she finds herself in the midst of an experience like the one that generated her idea in the first place. Inevitably she shares her enlarged horizon of possibilities with other members of her clan, first with some close friends and then, as word spreads, with groups of the curious. Gifted with powers of persuasion enlivened by what has been growing in her imagination, Genna convinces them, not to believe that what she has apparently encountered and is thinking about is real (they are far too sensible for that), but not to dismiss it. Indeed it might not be real, she admits to them; nevertheless, having only begun to explore the idea of such a reality, they must all equally say that it might well exist—nothing available to them clearly supports the thought that it does not. And if it is possible that so amazing a reality exists, then the very fact that it would be so amazing if it did exist reveals that careful attention to this possibility is required. Surely it would be very sad if it were real and yet they passed all their days oblivious to its existence, untouched by its power.

In time, some of Genna's friends and acquaintances undertake their own experiments with Genna's idea, making it their own, and beginning to experience the world differently in its light. They start gathering regularly, when life permits, often at the end of the day, to share their experiences and their reflections about the ultimate idea and how it is related to other ideas. They encourage one another in this form of life. And they work together to realize various forms of self-betterment and betterment of their community they are newly motivated to pursue because of their peculiar interaction, and because of the power of this thought of something deepest and best and also most surprising and transforming that has come to dominate their lives.

Thus far my story. It could be expanded in many ways. There are many endings. All I want to suggest in connection with it is this. If that story—or something like it—were discovered to be a true account of the early days on some planet science brought to our attention, we would most readily say of what is described in it that it marks *the beginnings of religion* on that planet. We would say this even though the conception of a Divine reality the planet's inhabitants are working with is left broad and generic, and even though the claim that there is such a reality is not believed.

But, you say, that was just a possible world. Yes, I reply, and in its very possibility we see a certain unexplored potential in the religious dimension of life that should influence us even as we mentally make our transition back to the actual. That religion has developed as it has in the actual world, with an emphasis on specific belief, is a purely contingent fact, and in thinking about other ways in which it might have developed we open windows to other, possibly better forms of religious practice in the present. Perhaps religion has had a bad start in the world. Maybe we have got ahead of ourselves in all our talk about specific, detailed beliefs concerning transcendent things, which keep us frozen in our places, our sectarian spaces, and prevent religion from moving forward.

Maybe religion needs to be born again.

6

Imagination is Key

The principles which ought to govern the cultivation and the regulation of the imagination—with a view on the one hand of preventing it from disturbing the rectitude of the intellect and the right direction of the actions and the will, and on the other hand of employing it as a power for increasing the happiness of life and giving elevation to the character—are a subject which has never yet engaged the serious consideration of philosophers. . . . And, I expect, that this will hereafter be regarded as a very important branch of study for practical purposes, and the more, in proportion as the weakening of positive beliefs respecting states of existence superior to the human, leaves the imagination of higher things less provided with material from the domain of supposed reality.

John Stuart Mill, *Three Essays on Religion*

Suppose that a philosopher came to visit Charles Darwin, say in the summer of 1863, catching him on a good day when he wasn't ill (Darwin was often ill that summer) or writing irritatedly to Asa Gray at Harvard about the American Civil War (in whose progress he was passionately interested). Suppose—a big supposition!—that this philosopher managed to lure Darwin away from the hothouse finished just that spring, where he loved "pottering over" plants, and engaged him in discussion.

Maybe it would take a very special philosopher to manage it. So—this is our story, after all—let's imagine that the philosopher is John Stuart Mill. In real life, the two never met. But they certainly knew of each other. The utilitarian Mill praised Darwin's theory of natural selection in his *System of Logic*. And Darwin, though ambivalent about the value of philosophizing, was well aware of Mill's stature. For by 1863,

Mill had reached the height of his fame as Britain's greatest living philosopher.

Although known as an atheist and as a severe critic of traditional religion—he didn't have to throw off religious belief, he tells us in his autobiography, because he "never had it"—Mill was at the time keeping quiet about his positive view of a form of "hopeful" religion, a view that was to be expressed briefly in his *Three Essays on Religion*, published posthumously. The idea of traditional theism, that there is an all powerful, all knowing, and all good creator of the universe, Mill believed to be false on account of the problem of evil. No compassionate deity with the power to prevent it would permit all the suffering and anguish of humankind. But an attitude of hope nourished by imaginative contemplation, he says in the *Essays*, can be reasonable when directed to the more limited idea of a finite but benevolent deity, struggling for the good of the world. This idea, unlike theism, cannot be shown to be *contrary* to fact. And taking it on board, mentally, through an exercise of imagination rather than belief, might be morally useful and thus commend itself to the conscientious utilitarian. "To me it seems that human life, small and confined as it is, and as, considered merely in the present, it is likely to remain even when the progress of material and moral improvement may have freed it from the greater part of its present calamities, stands greatly in need of any wider range and greater height of aspiration for itself and its destination, which the exercise of imagination can yield to it without running counter to the evidence of fact." These are ideas Mill already had in 1863, even though they were only published—and then without much development—in 1874.

Suppose that Mill hadn't kept quiet about all this. Suppose he had pioneered a study of the imagination and of how it may reasonably be utilized when belief seems impossible—a study he identifies in our epigraph as needing to be undertaken. Suppose all of Mill's ideas about religious imagination and hope had come up in a discussion between him and Darwin, a thinker as cautious and subtle and filled with humanitarian impulse as he, and been placed in the context of evolutionary thought. Might our Darwinian delay—the long stretch of time in which we've failed to see the relevance of *really* long stretches of time for religion—have been nipped in the bud? Might Mill have seen a link between the issues about imagination he was raising and the desirability of evolution beyond our present primitive state? Might Darwin, for his part, have become enthusiastic about the possible religious and philosophical consequences of his ideas, and when he came to write his own autobiography, have used a less narrow label than "Religious Belief" for the section on matters of faith?

It is of course impossible to say. But as I work out my own understanding of imaginative religion, the voices of these two thinkers in conversation may at times be overheard.

THE OBJECT OF FAITH

In the previous chapter I presented, with fairly broad brushstrokes, a new picture of an evolutionary form of religiousness. Its main features were religious diachronism, religious skepticism, religious developmentalism, and religious pragmatism. In this chapter, in further pursuit of the precision mentioned at the beginning of the last one, I offer some proposals as to how the practice of evolutionary religion might best be understood. No doubt other writers will have different ideas about this (and also additions or changes to suggest). The main thing is that some such discussion of religion-after-temporal-contextualization gets started and that our great evolutionary delay over matters religious be ended. But it may promote this end to have some specific proposals on the table. That is what I seek to provide in the present chapter.

These proposals can all be linked to the idea of *religious faith*. We've seen how, though traditionally regarded as indissolubly bound to belief, the attitude of faith may in a new incarnation appear as acceptance or assumption or something else again. There will be more on such alternatives in the next section. Here my focus is on the *object* of evolutionary faith, that to which it is directed—and I mean the central object. If we are going to have faith that _____ to guide all our religious activities, what proposition should fill the blank? Jews, Christians, and Muslims, for example, have traditionally professed faith that there is a loving and all-powerful personal God. What propositional counterpart can be suggested for evolutionary religion? Put otherwise, how should a bottom-line religious reality (or "Divine" reality, as I will sometimes say) be conceived by temporally contextualized religious beings?

In the last chapter I recommended intellectual minimalism on this issue. Detailed content for the concept in question ought, for good evolutionary reasons, to be avoided. But of course we don't want to go to the opposite extreme of saying nothing at all, or so little that there is hardly any way to distinguish religion from nonreligion.

This issue about *degree of content*—the extent to which the nature of the imagined religious reality ought to be specified—is one issue we need to settle. I'll refer to it as the question whether our concept of the Divine should be "thick" or "thin," with a thick concept offering details (for example, the personal details of theism) and a thin one only as much content as will identify it as a religious concept. But what content is that?

This question takes us back to Chapter 4, in which we tied religiousness to the idea of things that transcend the natural world. The central object of religious faith, the Divine as conceived by this or that religiousness, is going to include the notion of something more than or deeper than or greater than the world of physical nature explored by science. This is what we took "transcend" to imply. We also saw that such religious transcendence has several dimensions. To clarify what was said there, let's note that the religious will regard a Divine reality as something "more" not just (i) in factual terms but also (ii) in value and (iii) in what we might term importance, by which I mean its value for *us*. In philosophical terms: the first sort of transcendence is metaphysical transcendence, the second axiological transcendence, and the third soteriological transcendence. Notice that we haven't committed ourselves to the Divine reality being in any of these ways unlimited or ultimate (more on this in a moment); we're just trying to get clear about the basic religious idea of transcendence. To fill out a bit those three kinds of transcendence, we can say that if something is *metaphysically transcendent*, its existence is a fact distinct from any natural fact and in some way a more fundamental fact about reality than any natural fact. If something is *axiologically transcendent*, its intrinsic value—its splendour, its excellence—exceeds that of anything found in nature alone. And if something is *soteriologically transcendent*, then being rightly related to it will make for more well-being, fulfillment, wholeness, and the like for creatures than can naturally be attained. A Divine reality is supposed to be "more" in all three of these ways; it is regarded as transcendent not just metaphysically, but also axiologically and soteriologically. Call this *triple transcendence*.

Now back to my distinction between "thick" and "thin": if you say only that you conceive the Divine as triply transcendent and give no additional details as to the *nature* of its threefold transcendence, your concept remains thin. Otherwise it is thick. Let's make these definitions more conspicuous, because we'll be needing to refer to them from time to time:

Thick: a thick concept of the Divine says the Divine is triply transcendent *and also gives details* as to the nature of its threefold transcendence.

Thin: a thin concept of the Divine says that the Divine is triply transcendent and offers *no* additional details as to the nature of its transcendence.

So we have to decide whether the object of evolutionary faith should feature a concept of the Divine that is thick or thin. But there is also a second issue: how *deep* should we suppose those three sorts of transcendence to go—are they limited or unlimited? If transcendent, how far transcendent? Is the Divine also an ultimate reality in every respect, or is it perhaps less than that?

Now, perhaps an answer to these questions will be implied by the rest of what someone says when developing a religious concept thickly, but this need not be the case. Even if you give a lot of details as to the nature of the Divine—even if your concept is a thick one— those questions may remain unanswered. Mill, for example, put a fair bit of content into his revised religious idea: just as with the concept of the theistic God, we have the idea of a supernatural agent or person who forms intentions and acts accordingly—of course in service of the good. So Mill's concept is thick. But if all we know about it is what was just said, then we still don't know whether this Divine person of Mill's is limited or unlimited in the forms of transcendence it displays: is its existence not just a more fundamental fact about reality than any natural fact but the *most* fundamental? is it not just more intrinsically valuable than anything in nature but the *most* valuable possible? is it not just the source of more well-being than we could naturally attain but the source of our *deepest* good?

As a matter of fact, Mill never ultimizes as the second option in each of these questions does. His deity clearly doesn't have everything imaginable in depth of facticity, value, and importance, because for various reasons Mill thinks it wise to scale back the central religious concept from the standard theistic idea, which does seek to make the Divine absolutely unrestrictedly ultimate. Assuming we can see what the issue is here, I'll refer to it as the question whether our concept of the Divine should be "strong" or "weak," with a strong concept making the Divine unlimited or ultimate in all three spheres of transcendence and a weak one not doing so:

> **Strong:** a strong concept of the Divine says the Divine is *ultimate* in all three spheres of transcendence.
>
> **Weak:** a weak concept of the Divine says that the Divine is *not* in all three spheres ultimate.

So which way should our would-be practitioner of evolutionary religion jump on these issues? Should the religious idea she takes on board be thick or thin? Should it be strong or weak? Depending on how these notions are combined, we really have four options, which I will characterize as follows:

> **Thick/Strong:** a thick/strong concept of the Divine gives *details* as to the nature of its threefold transcendence and moreover regards the Divine as *ultimate* in all three ways.
>
> **Thick/Weak:** a thick/weak concept of the Divine gives *details* as to the nature of its threefold transcendence and holds that the Divine is *not* in all three ways ultimate.
>
> **Thin/Strong:** a thin/strong concept of the Divine gives *no* details as to the nature of its threefold transcendence, but regards the Divine as *ultimate* in all three ways.
>
> **Thin/Weak:** a thin/weak concept of the Divine gives *no* details as to the nature of its threefold transcendence and holds that the Divine is *not* in all three ways ultimate.

Theism provides a clear example of the first option, Thick/Strong. The theistic God has all power, all knowledge, all goodness, is the absolute Creator of the natural world, and our deepest good, so theists say, lies in being related to God in love. Both details and ultimacy are here. And notice that triple transcendence is here converted into *triple ultimacy*.

Mill's lesser deity we saw to provide an example of the second option, Thick/Weak. He held that demotion from ultimacy need not prevent an idea of transcendence from functioning perfectly well religiously. Others, such as his American contemporary William James (who was intellectually committed to some such notion) and the more recent Harvard philosopher Robert Nozick (who was not), have held similar views. And there are philosophers writing today who think this is or may be the right way to go.

Our third option, Thin/Strong, like theism, will embrace ultimacy, but will say less about it, holding only that the Divine is in some way metaphysically, axiologically, and soteriologically ultimate. So we still have triple ultimacy, on this option, but without any content added to that basic characterization.

Finally, a Thin/Weak concept of the Divine will be compatible with Mill's in saying that the Divine is less than ultimate metaphysically, axiologically, and soteriologically and will *also* have less content: no reference to the details of personhood appears here but only the basic content any such religion idea must have, namely the general idea of some kind of triple transcendence.

Having developed this framework for thinking about our two issues, let me say that for evolutionary religion I myself favor the second last of the options just mentioned: Thin/Strong. A thick religious concept, whether strong or weak, doesn't satisfy our condition of intellectual minimalism. On broadly evolutionary grounds I think we can say that even Mill's scaled-back version of the theistic idea has too much content. For it's all too easy, as thinkers such as Feuerbach and Freud and also the recently developed cognitive science of religion suggest, to extrapolate from *ourselves* when developing a concept of the Divine, and, in part for this reason, much too quick as well, in evolutionary terms. Let the filled out ideas of a person-like God or gods take their place alongside others, both actual and yet to be discovered, to be examined with equal care within a framework afforded by a much more *thinned out* religious concept. And let only the latter be *central* in evolutionary religion. Or so I would be inclined to say. The idea of a person—and indeed any idea similarly detailed— rules out other possibilities, other ways of filling out a religious picture, and we've already seen that evolutionary religion will want to keep as many such options open as possible.

So Thin is better than Thick. But I also think that Strong is better than Weak (if it seems I've cooked the books with my choice of terms, then feel free to substitute Skinny and Robust, Bold and Restrained). The most powerful religious experiences—like Genna's described at the end of the previous chapter—positively encourage totalization or ultimization in religious thought. The awe, wonder, and other numinous states elicited are unwilling to rest content with any characterization falling short of unlimited richness.

Now, the idea of a limited reality like Mill's deity might still be thought preferable because it will be more accessible to us. After all, you may say, we are thinking of ourselves as primitives here, so let's not overload our minds! But this only allows us to see another reason for favoring Strong over Weak. If evolutionary religion aims, among other things, to promote our evolution into a more mature state, it will need to *challenge* us. And the notion of a limited person—or indeed of a limited anything—does much less to challenge our imagination and encourage the stretching of our conceptual capacities than a strong idea might do (at least if that strong idea is also thin). Any form of religion appropriate to such an early stage of development as our own is well advised to emphasize "thinking big" when formulating its central idea—in part, as we'll see more fully in a later chapter, so as to facilitate enlarging ourselves. The religious idea needs to be big enough, surely, to embrace both reality and value. It needs to be *worthy* of our imaginations, and therefore must present to us more than the limited deity that, in a concession to the limits of popular imagination, Mill hesitantly advanced. It needs to be big enough that we—impressive creatures though we be—might exist at an extremely early stage in the discovery of its true dimensions.

Perhaps it's not a coincidence that not only theism but arguably all or most of today's religious traditions go Strong instead of Weak. When church bells call Christians to Sunday services, as they did a few moments ago in my seaside village while I was tramping through the nearby woods thinking about this chapter, they are not calling Christians to contemplate something of middling, perhaps consider-able, importance and value and depth of facticity. They are calling Christians to contemplate Something deemed to be of *ultimate* im-portance and value—inconceivably great—whose place in the nature of reality is ultimate too. (If you have any doubt about this, think about the word "worship" which appears in the typical reference to Christian services.)

But of course not only theistic forms of religion like Christianity are concerned with ultimate things. Theistic religion is an instance of a type, of which there are many other instances. The traditional idea of God shared by most Jews, Christians, and Muslims is a conception of something transcendent and ultimate, relationship with whom consti-tutes our highest good. But both monistic and dualistic Hindus say something similar about Brahman, while emphasizing the overriding importance of the religious path in one of its many possible forms as a way of finally securing release from the wheel of rebirth. And for Buddhists the idea of the Buddha-nature or of Nirvana and the emphasis on enlightenment through pursuit of the Noble Eightfold Path function in a similar fashion. Even forms of religion no longer practiced and apparently content with more limited realities, like ancient Greek religion, provide occasion for noticing the ultimistic idea. That idea is precisely what gives substance to the criticism of god-worship leveled at his fellow Greeks by the pre-Socratic philosopher Xenophanes, who pointed to flaws in the gods, suggesting that they were therefore unfit to be worshiped. The god he himself believes in, he says, is by contrast "one god, greatest among gods and men, in no way similar to mortals either in body or mind," a god who "sees all over, thinks all over, and hears all over." Very many forms of religion, both known and, one imagines, waiting to be discovered, engage in a mind-expanding conceptual totalization or ultimization, which is an activity tending toward the removal of all limitations from the object of concern. Should evolutionary religion do any less?

If you accept that rhetorical question, as I do, noting that evolutionary religion will need to find some place for powerful religious experiences and also remembering that it should challenge us, you will want the central concept we pick to be a strong one. If you also opt for a thin concept because of the investigative needs of primitive beings like us, then you're left with Thin/Strong, which is the idea of a reality triply ultimate, and that's all. Of course that's a lot! If my proposal were accepted, the fundamental idea of evolutionary religion would be an idea of something deepest in reality (metaphysically ultimate) that is also unsurpassably great (axiologically ultimate) and the source of our deepest good (soteriologically ultimate).

I call the claim that there is such a triply-ultimate reality *ultimism*. Be sure to note that this is not the name of a religion or way of practicing religion—as some have mistakenly thought on reading my work—but like the word "theism," only the name of a claim or proposition, the claim or proposition providing an object for evolutionary faith as I suggest we construe it. Ultimism is clearly a more general idea than theism, though entailed by it. Almost always in religious history it has been hidden inside some thicker claim like theism. I've been trying to coax it out into the open where we can look at it on its own. And the result is indeed a distinct option. (If Mill's idea was theism weakened, then ultimism is theism thinned.) Ultimism refers quite generally to the accessibility of an ultimate good springing from something ultimate in reality and value, rather than specifically to salvation found in a personal relationship with a perfect creator who loves us like a parent, or to any other extant religious details. Given its breadth and our immaturity, we must admit that ultimism may well be true (this follows also from the arguments of Chapter 4), even if we think that many existing attempts to fill it out, including traditional theism, are provably false. In part this is because many *other* detailed ways of filling it out may well remain undiscovered. Ultimism invites doubt rather than disbelief.

Notice that in satisfaction of a condition specified in the previous chapter, ultimism is set at a good distance from us, conceptually speaking: it is not so distant as to be incapable of touching us, but not so close and defined in its features as to potentially obscure alternatives and make us forget our place in time. And it is in the balance between these two things that its religious promise can be detected.

By "touching us" I mean primarily three things. We can be moved by what ultimism represents (although conventional religion is often much less interesting than a Dawkins-style naturalism, the central idea of evolutionary religion far transcends in emotive power his and any other non-ultimistic vision). We can even identify some of our religious experiences as possibly giving us some early form of contact with what it represents (instead of falling into premature identification of their object with what is depicted by one of the standard conceptions of existing religion). Furthermore, ultimism has enough content to provide a basis for judging what one ought to do—and so can function as a distinctively religious guide of behavior (as we'll see later in the chapter). By permitting investigation, I have in mind that ultimism is about as general a claim as one could adopt without leaving religion altogether—general enough, indeed, to permit investigation of all other strong religious claims, which represent the various ways of filling it out. We thus appear to have the best of both worlds. For we have a framework for ongoing religious investigation of the full array of more detailed strong religious claims, both actual and possible, to none of which one is committed, and also an available object of religious intellectual and emotional and practical commitment, *ultimism itself*—the smooth core, the capacious heart, of our most powerful religious visions.

THE ATTITUDE OF FAITH

Next let's try to think with a little more precision about what the *attitude* of faith should be—the attitude with which, in a dispensation of evolutionary religion, one might embrace such an idea as that of ultimism. Of course in religion-as-it-is the attitude is generally one of believing, but we have a mandate to think beyond belief.

In Chapter 3 we noticed that not everyone analyzes belief the same way. There appears to be agreement, however, that there belongs to belief some component that is fundamentally involuntary and fully engaged in a sense that implies learning of the falsehood of the proposition expressing one's belief would normally make for surprise. (Imagine learning that you didn't lock your car door or that your wife is home, when you had believed otherwise.) Earlier I spoke of this component quite generally as the "sense of reality." And although not everyone analyzes faith *without* belief the same way either, there is a common emphasis on *the absence of that involuntary component and a different sort of mental engagement.* The experience that goes with belief is now replaced by something more voluntary, such as assumption or acceptance or explicit trust—something such that although disappointment may still be felt if the proposition in question turns out to be false, surprise normally will not. (This time imagine learning that you didn't lock your door when you only decided to trust that you had.)

It is also agreed on (almost) all sides that nonbelieving faith is not reducible to—is something more than—propositional *hope.* The attitude of hope-that, at least as normally construed, is weaker, less assertive than faith-that, and quite involuntary. If you only hope that you locked the door, you may not be able to get the question off your mind, whereas either belief or voluntary trust will allow you to put it behind you mentally. (Hope, it could be said, is intellectually bittersweet: constantly taking away with one hand what it gives with the other.) I suppose further discussion must determine which, if any, of the conceptions of nonbelieving faith mentioned here and in the previous chapter is best. I rather suspect they represent different ways of having faith nonbelievingly. But by reflecting further on any of them, a more finegrained understanding of that notion will potentially become available.

Let me now develop my favorite conception of nonbelieving faith, like Mill emphasizing the role of imagination (though not in a way limited to hope, as we normally experience it). In a collection of recent essays called *The Architecture of the Imagination*, editor Shaun Nichols reports a near-consensus in psychology and philosophy of psychology that propositional imagination or imagining-that (for example, imagining that *a mouse is running across the floor in the next room*) is "a distinct cognitive attitude (DCA)," that is, an attitude distinct from belief. In particular, it is functionally distinct: "imaginings are distinguished from beliefs by their pattern of causal interaction." When you imagine something that you don't believe to be true, you won't immediately act accordingly, as you tend to do when you believe it. Imagining the mouse coming for you, you won't immediately leap onto a chair or reach for the broom. But, interestingly, the emotions are affected similarly: Nichols provides lots of evidence that "the affective response to imagining a scenario closely tracks the affective response that would occur if the subject came to believe that the scenario was real." Here too thinking about the mouse is confirmatory! In one of the essays Nichols has collected, by Timothy Schroeder and Carl Matheson, we even learn from neuroscientific investigations just what's going on in the brain when all of this is happening, with the imaginative representation "sending impulses to emotional centers like the orbitofrontal cortex, affective stratium, and amygdala" in much the same way that propositional belief does. Still, what we have here is a DCA, with children as young as two easily able to keep imagined worlds apart from the one thought to be real (Nichols reminds us that even hungry children don't try to eat their mud pies) and able to avoid slipping from imagination into belief.

These recent investigative results should be kept in mind as I link imagination and faith. Can imagination really support *emotions* of the sort we would want to think of as capable of being felt or cultivated by a religious person? Yes, indeed. In fact, when we see that imaginative faith is not a matter of pretense or "make believe," which implies thinking the relevant proposition *false*, but rather a response to uncertainty, the possibility of religious emotions without religious belief is all the more clear. Can we prevent imagination from slipping into belief? Certainly, especially if the one having imaginative faith is an adult who continually reminds herself (or is continually reminded by the world) of how weak *evidential* support for the relevant proposition remains. What we're talking about here is indeed a DCA.

So how, in my view, can this DCA, imagining-that, provide a way of understanding what it is to have faith in a nonbelieving way? Well, first let me say that in agreement with pretty much everyone else who has written on this subject, I would say faith without belief is realized in circumstances where you don't believe the relevant proposition (call it p) but (1) you nonetheless think it would be *good* for p to be true—here's what philosophers call a "pro-attitude"—and (2) you take p to be epistemically possible, holding that it can't reasonably be *dis*believed either. Faith is indeed compatible with skepticism, but disbelief would be hard to reconcile with it, psychologically or rationally. And now let's add to those two conditions three more: in that skeptical or doubting state, although you're not being involuntarily represented-*to* in the manner of belief, (3) you deliberately represent or picture the world *to yourself* through the power of the imagination as including the truth of p. Moreover (4) you form the intention to be mentally guided by this picture on an ongoing basis when relevant things come up, that is, to think accordingly and as a matter of policy; and (5) you follow through on this policy. (Of course such a policy may have a longer or shorter duration depending on the nature of p and the nature of the practical reasons to which you respond.) Notice that the policy here is still purely intellectual, concerning how you will *think*; we haven't yet got to the distinct matter of how, more generally, your behavior may be adjusted accordingly.

Something you *won't* do when you have faith in this way—at least if you're honest—is tell anyone that you believe that p. Nor will you tell *yourself* this; or tell yourself anything else designed to produce belief. Things may seem to be otherwise when you notice that to keep the relevant picture—the one reported by p—properly before your mind, you may need to repeat the proposition in question to yourself, perhaps quite enthusiastically! But this isn't any kind of self-deception, as can be seen in the example of a runner laboring in the race, unsure if he can win. When he keeps going in imaginative faith, repeatedly saying to himself "Yes, I will make it! Yes, I will make it!," he isn't rightly seen as making some kind of inner *claim*. He doesn't represent himself as believing the proposition in question to himself any more than to the runner beside him. No falsehood or self-deception is expressed or perpetrated. The inner declarative sentences are rather a way of bringing or keeping the imagined state of affairs before his mind and express an intention to ongoingly direct his mind accordingly.

Here's another example. Think of having imaginative faith that your once drug addicted daughter, with several relapses in her not-so-distant past, will prove reliable when you give her the keys to your car and she drives away. If you manage to achieve this condition, I suggest, you will remain relatively calm, mentally, even though a questioner could elicit from you the admission that you don't *believe* she will be reliable. Though you don't believe this, you do think the relevant proposition epistemically possible and of course you have a pro-attitude toward it. And you are allowing your associated mental behavior to be structured by, *disciplined* by, the corresponding imagined picture, which you bring before your mind as needed, mentally nodding your head throughout the evening.

Clearly what we have here is more than hope, at least as normally construed (though it may well include or presuppose hope, via the pro-attitude). Recalling what was said above about the DCA, we should remind ourselves that it isn't belief, and needn't turn into belief. At times, as when less effort is involved because imagination is kept aloft by the attractiveness of what is imagined (or by the reinforcement provided by deliberately acting on what is thus imagined), such imaginative *faith* that p may easily be confused with *belief* that p. But one can tell that it's not belief by considering how well p appears to be evidentially supported in those circumstances, or by considering what the reaction would be were p to be judged false—surprise or disappointment?

Is it then reducible to acceptance? Not really. Acceptance involves taking a proposition mentally on board *and* being disposed to act on it, whereas here we're just talking about the former—the cognitive or thinking side of things. (We'll bring the other side into our discussion in a moment.) Besides, you could accept something—say, a scientific hypothesis you're studying at school—even if you didn't have any pro-attitude towards the idea that it's true. Faith, unlike acceptance, entails a pro-attitude: the idea of having *faith* that something *bad* will happen doesn't make any sense.

I've used a couple of secular examples of imaginative faith. But of course it's to religion that I want to apply the notion. Darwin himself, I suspect, whether because of an anxious personality or simply the stubborn opacity of nature, was frequently called upon to exercise such imaginative faith in non-religious contexts: faith, in his early career, that a mechanism to account for the origin of species would be found; faith that his book describing that mechanism would survive the hot blasts unleashed against it; faith that his theory's gaps, such as the missing origin for the variations leading ultimately to species, would in time be filled. Yet when, in later life, Darwin responded to letters about *religious* faith, he always intimated that it was unavailable to him, because—so he repeatedly explained his condition—he had found nothing to keep him in a state of *belief,* to prevent him from being an agnostic. (As this suggests, Darwin was also pretty narrowly focused on theism as the only relevant object of faith.)

Here Darwin's imagination—imagination about imagination—failed him. Actually, not much imagination is required to deliver the vital insight. If we consider the short distance we have travelled, in evolutionary terms, and the little we may presently be able to discern about profound things, while also noticing how, from a distance, a religious proposition like ultimism can inspire us, it may seem simple common sense that a religious response appropriate to our time must be animated by something like imagination rather than by belief. Ultimate things of the sort spoken of by religion certainly should appeal to the imaginations of finite creatures seeking to grow beyond primitivity, but precisely because of our primitivity, cannot be taken on board with an easy confidence. Nonetheless when we see how the very imagination just mentioned allows for an *alternative* form of faith, perhaps we'll put 1 and 1 together and get 2. (Faith 2.0?)

Mill, as we have seen, got a little closer to 2. But even he appears to have made the assumption that a full-blooded faith attitude must be believing, since he chooses for the possible nonbelieving attitude he describes not the label "faith," which might otherwise have seemed the obvious choice, but rather "hope." Mill's assumption is false, as we've seen. And in any case, much more than hope, in any ordinary sense, is present when one has imaginative faith-that—and certainly when one acts in light of it, not just mentally but in other ways too, thus turning one's faith *that* there is an Ultimate into faith *in* the Ultimate and a full religious life.

Imaginative religious faith, understood not as a stop-gap measure but as an attitude with vital integrity and vibrancy of its own, might be precisely the right attitude to direct toward ultimism at our present stage of development even if belief is not, and even if for evolutionary reasons it is something we shouldn't apply to a more detailed religious proposition like theism. Here, I suggest, we have a response that can keep religion afloat and indeed lead it into more interesting waters, away from the dangers of immaturity so often bound up with the psychological features of belief. Such imaginative faith, especially if directed toward ultimism, is an attitude of the most unrestricted and unrestricting sort. It is perfectly compatible with doubting nonbelief and indeed entails nonbelief. It is content with possibility. As noted in the last chapter, we are not yet ready for belief and so we should *look for* an attitude other than belief to characterize religion at our early stage of development. Imaginative faith, so I suggest, fits this description admirably. It is a faith for beings who wish to experiment with a fuller maturity, willing to sweat their way to enlightenment—to show others and themselves what they're really made of.

THE LIFE OF FAITH

So what *would* such a life have to show for itself? It's time to transition from evolutionary faith as a way of thinking about or seeing the world (faith *that* there is a transcendent reality) to a new dimension so far just suggested, the added level that would be required to turn such faith into a form of life, which is a disposition to act in light of what one sees (faith *in* the transcendent). If the proposition in question is ultimism, then the actions done will involve acting on its content: cultivating the patterns of behavior that would be appropriate if it—together with everything else one has believingly or otherwise taken on board—were true.

But perhaps you'll think that the idea of a triply ultimate reality, if left thin, could hardly *have* much in the way of robust emotional consequences or consequences for behavior. Well, let's take a look. In having faith that ultimism is true, I train my thought on the idea that what is deepest in the nature of things is also unsurpassably the greatest and that its wonders are in some way transformatively accessible to me and to the world. (This may seem quite unbelievable but remember that I don't believe it—I am *imagining* things to be so. Moreover, being temporally contextualized, recognizing my primitivity and the need for evolutionary skepticism, I don't *dis*believe it either, and so am prevented from discarding such an exercise as obviously unrealistic.) Though not experiencing the involuntary rush of belief, I have put this idea in charge of my mental life. Notice that in so doing I also take on board all its logical entailments or implications. The logical implications of a proposition like ultimism are propositions that have to be true if it is, thus any picture of the world governed by ultimism has to make room for them. They can be exposed using "if–then" expressions.

For example, if ultimism is true, then there is a reality transcendent of the natural world and the scientifically law-abiding world of nature isn't all there is. If it's true, then metaphysical naturalism—which claims there is no such transcendent reality—is false. If ultimism is true, then indeed it is the dimension of reality transcending nature that is most fundamental and important. If it is true, then the core of reality is on the side of the good, and may indeed in some sense *be* the good. If it is true, then—even though we might have a hard time seeing exactly how—the universe or our environment in the largest sense is not indifferent to our deepest needs. If ultimism is true, furthermore, then it is through associating ourselves with the reality of which it speaks that we can best make contact with value. If it is true, then given the obvious fact of deeply damaged Earthly lives or Earthly lives cut short, there must be some sort of second chance for at least some of us. (For there is clearly no possible world in which a child whose life is filled with suffering and then cut short has already achieved all that "soteriological ultimacy" could sensibly be claimed to include for her.) If ultimism is true, moreover, then anxiety and acquisitiveness are equally shortsighted. If it is true, then taking risks for the sake of the good is appropriate, aligning us as it does with the deepest nature of reality, instead of foolhardy. If it is true, then the sort of inquiry that, if successful, will bring us to the deepest understanding of the world is religious in nature. And so on.

More could indeed be said about what ultimism logically implies, but already we should be able to sense the practical consequences of the propositions piling up here for primitive creatures like us who decide to take them on board, mentally, and also to act accordingly. Let's look at these more closely. I suggest that what is emerging is a distinctive and attractive sort of evolutionary religiousness featuring at least three "dimensions" or "directions": *downward* (into an understanding of ultimate things), *inward* (into ourselves, with the aim of shaping, and perhaps reshaping, our fundamental dispositions), and *outward* (into the world and an engagement with its needs). Let's take these in turn.

1. *Downward*. Remember that we're working within an evolutionary perspective that in some ways reverses our usual view of things: we must suppose ourselves to be at the beginning, not the end of a long process of religious intellectual and spiritual development. And if value is embodied most fully by the fundamental reality of which ultimism speaks, then, given our relative ignorance, one way of facilitating contact with this value must involve coming to *understand*

it better, spreading our roots through all the Earth in search of such understanding. Religious inquiry (inquiry concerning religion) is in this way turned into *religious* inquiry (inquiry that instantiates religion). Indeed, evolutionary religion comes to have an attractive dimension that is denied many traditional forms of faith, which suppose that a fully deep and correctly detailed understanding have already been reached and are attached to it by the mental glue of belief. Here, instead, we have "faith seeking understanding" in its purest form.

How can this deepened understanding be pursued? Well, there are, in this case, no scriptures and no established rituals, passed down to us from the (so-called) ancients, that we can unquestioningly treat as authoritative and reliable. But precisely because of this, because of our admitted ignorance, the religious person must expect that any experience at all, whether on one's own or with others, and indeed whether outside traditional religion's doors or within, may lead to insights of the greatest importance. Notice that inquiry is therefore, at least potentially, infused with an excitement it would otherwise lack. We should be open to learning about value in unexpected places and having our ideas about value expanded or changed in unexpected ways. Every stitch and fold in the fabric of our lives is included here—not just "religious experience" as standardly construed but the needs, capacities, and experiences associated with eating, drinking, sleeping, thinking, lovemaking, conversation, traveling, building, caring for animals, illnesses, and a thousand other "ordinary" things. Ignorance can feed religion, and, in a manner analogous to what one finds in Buddhist teachings, emptiness can be fullness of an unexpected sort.

Now, such openness and meditative attentiveness, together of course with more structured study (in various forms of religious studies as well as at the intersection between religion and such things as science, art, and philosophy), may not immediately yield detailed results of the sort claimed by traditional believers. Findings shared in groups of the imaginatively religious may well be preliminary, and will be seen, at least initially, as epistemic possibilities to be set alongside other epistemic possibilities; but in arriving at them, religious persons are acting on ultimism, whose content they imaginatively appropriate, and more specifically are acting on an aim to deepen our understanding of ultimate things.

One more point. As I've suggested, it's natural to think of the attitude cultivated by the religious person as she concerns herself with all these facets of inquiry as fundamentally a *meditative* attitude. One shouldn't suppose, however, that this implies any undue solemnity; religious insight, for the skeptically imaginative, may come from entering fully into wit and humor or flights of fancy as much as from any other experience.

2. *Inward.* The second dimension or direction of an evolutionary faith response leads us into *ourselves* with the aim of shaping or reshaping some of our most fundamental dispositions. As limited, vulnerable human beings at an early stage of evolution, our lives may often seem fragmented, resisting significant unity; we may easily lose focus and despair of fundamental order and meaning. But as we saw earlier, it is written into ultimism and its implications that there is a fundamental pattern of meaning and order in things, and the religious person is therefore called to "get it together:" using ultimism as a point of stability, she boldly orders her life in accordance with what she sees when she imagines it true, courageously navigating through apparent chaos with its support on her mind.

Here too ignorance and limitation may be helpful, and sources of unexpected delight. As the Taoists have taught us, the complexities of reality are such that there may be a huge variety of ways in which what appear as infinitely knotted problems are capable of dissolving into new and meaningful perspectives which add layers of depth to one's life. In evolutionary faith one is constantly teaching oneself to be more open to such things, to look for them, to expect them, and to take advantage of them when they appear. A certain patience as well as a sensitive, discriminating awareness might be expected to be among the results.

Limited, vulnerable human beings also already have, at a pretty fundamental level, such dispositions as impulsive acquisitiveness and anxiety. The dampening of such dispositions and their replacement over time by such things as long-term thinking and self-control, modest contentment, and serenity are further goals set before us by ultimism, since, as was earlier noted, given the truth of that proposition, acquisitiveness and anxiety are objectively shortsighted. And we will train ourselves not to grasp at limited goods of the moment, as if they appear just by chance and must swiftly be seized before all opportunity to participate in goodness is gone, but instead to put ourselves on the line for the sake of possibly deeper and more enduring goods.

So there is "inner work" to be done by someone who commits to a faith response to ultimism. Regularly putting *herself* into the picture she holds before her mind and allowing it to absorb or refashion her less mature concerns, acting in accord with the more mature self to which she is momentarily "boosted," she is able to establish new and corresponding patterns of thought, emotion, and physical activity.

Some practical examples: How important, if I am a person of ultimistic faith, is my frustrated desire to have a new instead of a used car or computer? How fearful (i.e. worthy of fear) are the illnesses that beset me? After all, I am having faith that much deeper and richer and more interesting things are afoot in the world than the possibility of driving around in a new car, and indeed, "driving around" might largely be *instrumentally* valuable in relation to those deeper things; thus I should seek to be content with the used car or computer I can afford, so long as it is serviceable. And I am having faith that ultimately all will be well; so I should seek to train myself to resist the disconcerting—and distracting—thoughts and behaviors to which illness can give rise.

All of this can of course be very difficult, but it is possible, and even its difficulties only give new meaning (and plausibility!) to the idea of religious faith as virtuous or meritorious. In any case, the point being defended here—that a skeptical-imaginative faith response has clearly specifiable practical content and interesting substance—is powerfully assisted by these ideas about the inner life.

3. *Outward*. It was noted earlier that if ultimism is true, then what might otherwise appear as unduly risk-taking behavior on behalf of the good in fact only more fully aligns us with the deepest nature of reality. It follows that we act on our faith that ultimism is true if we leave our comfort zone and move out into a world still rich in chaos and calamity, involving ourselves in (what would be called) risk-taking behavior on behalf of the good when the opportunity to do so arises. For example, a band of the imaginatively religious, like people sent out by the Mennonite Central Committee, a Christian organization, might respond positively and resolutely to an opportunity to be of use in difficult parts of the world—say, to an invitation to aid in reconstruction efforts in Afghanistan—instead of allowing themselves to be deterred by fear or by other self-serving rationalizations grounded in short-term concerns. Or I might submit, with similar resolution, to medical experimentation in the final stages of a terminal illness that promises to bring me much pain but likely will contribute to the healing of many in the future.

But why, someone may ask, should faith that ultimism is true be thought to make risk-taking behavior of the sort I have described appropriate, rather than *complacency*? After all, everything is going to come out ok in the end, isn't it? Why should I feel called to put myself on the line for something that will be taken care of in *any* event?

This objection forgets that ultimistic religion, insofar as it aims to be rational, is taken up within a more general framework suitable to early inquiry that allows belief of such things as intuitively obvious and psychologically unavoidable moral principles, among which are some bidding us to involve *ourselves* in resisting evil. Belief of such principles, in conjunction with imaginative faith that ultimism is true, must surely prepare us to imagine that something can be done about the horrors around us, and invite us to put our shoulders to the wheel. But the criticism also reflects a somewhat undernourished understanding of the religious role and value of risk-taking behavior on behalf of the good. The latter's point comes not just from the fact that it helps to "get things done"—though getting things done will obviously appeal to someone who takes up a religious commitment with moral sensitivity. It also represents a way of seeking to deepen one's connectedness to any deeper reality there may be—a way of seeking to align one's own powers and propensities with those one imagines to be operative, at the deepest level, in the nature of things. And is there any better way of seeking to deepen one's relation to a mysterious reality axiologically and soteriologically ultimate than by seeking to further the good precisely where it seems most stubbornly hidden or absent?

But what, the objector may continue, is to prevent the risk-taking behavior a religious person selects from being rather more troubling than those I have mentioned in my examples? Might it not instead involve something like, oh, say, flying airplanes into towers? The point is that if we lack, in ultimism, detailed content ruling some actions out and others in, perhaps only a partisan (in this case, North American liberal) bias will lead us to suppose that we know what sort of risk-taking behavior to cultivate.

However this point is guilty of a kind of level confusion: it confuses the recognition that risk-taking behavior on behalf of the good is called for with a specification of *which specific actions should be taken*. In recognizing the relevance of the former, we already contribute to a more precisely defined evolutionary religiousness, which is my goal. We don't need the latter for this purpose. Notice how we will take some Taoist or Buddhist or Christian form of religion to have a clear and distinct shape even while allowing for disagreement among practitioners of that form of religion about (for example) how exactly one should meditate or pray. The same thing applies here.

But we shouldn't just ignore specific and troubling actions of the sort cited by the objection. They, too, can be linked with our immaturity, and we need some clear reassurance that the new religious way here explored will not simply lead us down the more disconcerting paths associated with the old. I'd suggest that we can deal with this issue by noticing that harmful terrorist acts (and other actions relevantly like them), done in the name of religion, arise from a much narrower range of considered information, and from much narrower loyalties, than consistent practitioners of evolutionary religion could, given their evolutionary skepticism, ever find appealing. In a sense, and ironically, it is precisely *because* our skeptics are disposed to allow less detail into their cognitive commitments that the sort of risk-taking behavior we might expect from them is not of this sort. Also present and influential in the troubling cases, one suspects, is confident religious belief—belief sufficiently confident to override the normal influence of common moral principles—and thus an attitude incompatible with skeptical *faith*. Once more we see how our ignorance makes it easier to prove that ultimistic faith has clear and substantial and attractive practical implications instead of harder.

RELIGIOUS COMMUNITY

I want to conclude these opening proposals as to what religion-after-temporal-contextualization might look like by showing how the sort of evolutionary religiousness I have been describing need not be unduly individualistic but instead can accommodate what is most appealing about religious community. One way of seeing this involves noticing that, in such religiousness, we can readily find not just the three dimensions or directions already distinguished above, reflecting an extension and significant enlargement (appropriate to our stage of evolutionary development) of the concerns of any sensitive moral agent, but also two distinct levels. For in the imaginative skeptic's religious life we will have, first of all, the actions and dispositions that would immediately reflect the content of her faith in ways already mentioned, and then, secondly, the actions and dispositions she performs or cultivates *in order to make actions and dispositions at the first level easier, more natural, or stronger.* (And so, for example, she will look for things she can do to ward off laziness, inattentiveness, lack of focus, superficiality, and narrowness of vision.)

Development at this second level is obviously appropriate, given knowledge of our limited selves, if ultimism is true, and represents another goal that the imaginative skeptic acting on ultimism will pursue. And here religious community must present itself as a vital mechanism. Members of such a community can of course support one another in a multitude of ways in the forms of investigation, self-formation, and risk-taking behavior that we have found at the first level of the religious life. And the more tight-knit the community—the deeper and thicker the layers of connective tissue, intellectual, social, moral, and emotional, joining its members to each other—the more effective religious community will be in this role.

But the importance of religious community goes far beyond its instrumental value. It has the great advantage of providing a context in which *everything* we've said about evolutionary religion in an imaginative mode can be integrated and unified. Community-mindedness and collaborative thinking will more and more be a part of the skeptically imaginative religious person's perspective. And certainly her community and the people in it and her various overlapping relations with them will more and more come to be valued deeply for their own sakes, as she makes progress with our three dimensions or directions of faith. Seeking to fashion one's dispositions in accordance with the content of ultimism means, as we have seen, movement away from egoistic, self-centered concern. And looking for value in unexpected places, one will surely find it in all the frustrating but at the same time fascinating twists and turns of other minds. In any case, it's hard to imagine the ultimate good for human beings promised by ultimism's soteriological aspect being detached from the intrinsically valued and valuable quality of life-with-others available in such a religious community.

Now, everything I have said so far is compatible with the following conception of religious community: nonbelievers who have no connection to traditional religion but nonetheless see value in exercising their imaginations and acting in the ways I have described band together for such things as mutual emotional and physical support and encouragement, ultimism-related study, and the facilitating of deeper, richer experience, as well as collective action to further the good. I see no problem with this, and perhaps if evolutionary skepticism were to spread in conjunction with the gestalt shift about religion needed to end our imaginative blight, religious faith would more and more come to take on such a complexion as we begin the next 10,000 years.

But I want to point out how there is nothing in my picture of evolutionary religion to prevent nonbelievers who once were believers of one stripe or another from enriching their brand of religious community with elements from the religious traditions with which they most identify. One can imagine former Christian believers metaphorizing the specific doctrines of one Christian denomination or another, allowing (for example) figures of dying and rising to permeate their new religiousness, in the context of a broader imaginative faith that the framework proposition of ultimism is quite literally true. Here evolutionary religion meets radical Christian theology, for many theologians are heavily invested in metaphorization (though not always with a clear sense of what makes it an authentically religious activity, or how far to take it). Similar stories could be told about the psychological appropriation of the often complex relations among Hinduism's gods or the physical and psychological appropriation of Taoist exercises or Buddhist meditation.

The great benefit of evolutionary religion is that, unencumbered by narrower and belief-based traditional loyalties, its adherents can regard *all* of these forms as compatible and operating in perfect harmony—as different *styles* of one skeptical-imaginative evolutionary religiousness. Indeed, because we are exploring all the cracks and crevices of the world, rejoicing in its diversity and richness, there will be encouragement rather than disparagement of the proliferation of different styles of evolutionary religion, and of the building of networks of intercommunication among them.

These may seem unrealistic aspirations, *especially* for our immature stage of development! But it's interesting to notice that incipient forms of them are being realized already. The journalist Winifred Gallagher's explorations of pluralistic and "neoagnostic" religious trends in her book *Working on God* include a description of how a Jewish synagogue in New York City is sharing space with a Methodist church, and how the two communities have forged a mutually respectful interfaith partnership. Other examples may be found in Diana L. Eck's *Encountering God: A Spiritual Journey from Bozeman to Banaras.* Eck is a religious studies scholar and director of the Pluralism Project at Harvard University. As she writes: "Imaging a wider *we* does not mean leaving our separate communities behind, but finding increasingly generative ways of living together as a community of communities. To do this, we all must imagine together who *we* are." Evolutionary religion offers a new framework within which to think about this question.

* * *

John Stuart Mill, in the passage I have made my epigraph in this chapter, gestures at the possibility of a more mature imaginative religion *after* skepticism, and it is true, as he says there, that it has "never yet engaged the serious consideration of philosophers." Mill speaks of the need for principles: perhaps if he had been able to engage the subject more deeply, he would have seen the relevance of his contemporary Darwin's evolutionary thinking.

Perceptive readers will no doubt notice that in my attempt, in the pair of chapters concluded here, to bring out this relevance and develop some "principles" while staying focused on imagination, there is some overlap with religion *before* skepticism—with traditional religious practices, or practices associated with them. Should this lead us to question just how new evolutionary religion is? In one sense, perhaps. But in another and more important sense, not at all. A more interesting insight awaits. What we should notice is that the most important practical imperatives associated with religious views *tend to stem from their more general implications*, which are widely shared, and often bound up with the content of ultimism. So when focusing on ultimism alone, we should *expect* to see an overlap of sorts with traditional religion. Since at the same time the particularities of more detailed religious claims and their often troubling practical consequences are left behind, we again appear to have the best of both worlds: continuity with religion as the world has seen it so far and a chance for some of its most attractive general goals and practices to endure, but also clear motivation to be pushing forward, constantly forward, toward all that only the future may reveal of what is most beautiful, good, and true.

7

The "Chief Objections"

Such is the sum of the several chief objections and difficulties which may justly be urged against my theory.... I have felt these difficulties far too heavily over many years to doubt their weight. But it deserves especial notice that the more important objections relate to questions on which we are confessedly ignorant; nor do we know how ignorant we are.

Charles Darwin, *On the Origin of Species*

Robert Nozick once wrote that "the word *philosophy* means the love of wisdom, but what philosophers really love is reasoning." And what philosophers reason about more than almost anything else is the weight of objections to their views. There are no crucial experiments in philosophy. But the ability of a philosopher to show through careful reasoning that there are answers to objections is something like the ability of a scientist to make successful predictions. We might even say that a philosopher who confidently presents his case is making the "prediction" that objections to it will be answerable. You can bet he's tracked down a lot of them. Indeed, he may have traveled from conference to conference assiduously collecting them! Following a practice my students find perverse or masochistic (or sadistic, when they are asked to learn it), he has probably spent hours devising fiendishly clever forms of opposition to his own view, so that by proving even the strongest challenges unsuccessful, he may convincingly claim to have come out on top—or on good days, to be approaching wisdom.

Though not a philosopher, Charles Darwin was well aware of the power of objections. In *On the Origin of Species*, which sported no decisive experiment and which he himself called "one long argument," Darwin patiently and charitably developed a variety of arguments against the theory of evolution by natural selection and carefully answered them all. By doing so, he was able to show that his theory passed a large number of tests and that his own argument deserved a careful hearing.

In the present chapter, the first of the book's final pair, I too am concerned with objections, as I turn from the explanation of evolutionary religion to its defense. Now, some problems and criticisms are going to be coming up quite naturally in the next chapter, and I'll address them there in the course of developing positive arguments for my views. But there are a few basic objections—"chief" objections—that I want to deal with before turning to those arguments, so they don't distract us when we do. And since reasoning that successfully challenges the specific proposals of the previous chapter might leave the more general proposals of Chapter 5 untouched and the general idea of evolutionary religion unharmed, I will concentrate here on dialectical arrows that, uninterrupted, could reach both of the chapters in the previous pair.

Some of the chief objections to my proposals, as we'll see, like those Darwin considered, are related to "questions on which we are confessedly ignorant." Furthermore, the effects of temporal contextualization are such that, more than once, we will, like him, be forced to admit that "we do not know how ignorant we are."

DOES EVOLUTIONARY RELIGION SUCCUMB
TO THE PROBLEM OF EVIL?

I start with two rather fundamental objections, which attempt to overthrow evolutionary religious skepticism by showing that religious claims are all false. In other words, these objections defend what I have called irreligious belief, or religious disbelief. Of course, if we should disbelieve all religious claims, then it's hard to see how it could be reasonable to be religious in any way, shape, or form—even an evolutionary one.

The first objection tries to massage the old problem of evil into such a devastating result. How might this be done? Well, the best bet for the objector will be to combine clear facts about horrific cruelty and suffering in the world with claims and inferences sanctioned by rational intuition—anything else, I suggest, is likely to run into the problem of Total Evidence. This means that the critic should favor a style of reasoning that has quite often been used in arguments against traditional theism: an argument attempting to establish *logical inconsistency* between some set of religious claims and the facts about evil.

Here's how such an argument might run in our evolutionary context. There's obviously a lot of horrific cruelty and suffering in the world, and by adding to your world-picture the deep past, in which evolutionary processes over millions of years have sacrificed billions of creatures on the altar of biological fitness, you only make things a lot worse. Someone whose religiousness is in any way evolutionary has to take all this on board. And she has to take it on board *together with* the idea that there is a triply transcendent reality, whose place in reality is deeper and whose value and importance are greater than that of anything in nature. These things, so it may be said, *don't* go together, logically. Whatever the transcendent may be, it can't help getting its hands rather dirty at least metaphorically. It would appear to be at any rate a partial cause of things being as bad as they are, since evil is *everywhere* among us, and if metaphysically transcendent, its existence is supposed to afford a deeper-than-natural explanation of what goes on at any rate *somewhere* in nature. Yet it is also assumed to be deeply and transcendently splendid and excellent, and being aligned with it is regarded as being better for *us*—for creatures in the world—than any mundane benefit. How could these things be the case? That is, given what metaphysical transcendence implies about its role in the production of evil, it seems unbelievable that the reality in question could *also* be axiologically and soteriologically transcendent. But if it couldn't, then the adherent of evolutionary religion in any form is caught in a contradiction when she has skeptical faith that there is a triply transcendent reality. And one's response to a contradiction should not be skepticism! It ought to be disbelief.

Such a statement of the problem may at first appear impressive. But to see the problem with this problem of evil, one need only consider how weakly I was forced to phrase things, when developing it, given our new temporalist context of reasoning. I couldn't say that the triply transcendent reality is necessarily a *being*, much less a person-like being: an advocate of evolutionary religion, as we've seen, has reason to select a thin religious concept rather than a thick one including such notions. Moreover, since an adherent of evolutionary religion might disagree with me about ultimism and go Thin/Weak instead of

Thin/Strong, I was able to say only that the triply transcendent has to be taken as affording a deeper explanation than could naturally be provided of what goes on at any rate somewhere in nature. I couldn't say that it has to be regarded as metaphysically ultimate, affording a deeper-than-natural explanation of *everything* natural. Anyone countenancing Thin/Weak can say that perhaps not all laws of nature *have* a deeper explanation, in which case our transcendent reality has to put up with them just as we do. Or perhaps something else explains some of those laws. Or perhaps something metaphysically ultimate (though axiologically and soteriologically irrelevant) explains the existence and behavior of the more limited but religiously relevant transcendent reality responsible for part of nature; and thus that *other* and metaphysically ultimate reality provides the *deepest* explanation of why nature takes the shape it does, both there and elsewhere. The point is that it's a problem for our objector that all of these suggestions are compatible with religious faith in an evolutionary context, since an impressive problem of evil will grow only from a commitment more definite.

Well, you may respond, this really isn't the case: as the argument I've constructed has it, even responsibility for how things go *somewhere* in nature is a problem for religious faith since evil is *everywhere* among us. But now we're in a position to see the main problem with the objector's argument (there are others I won't go into, such as the fact that "somewhere" might be somewhere *else* in the universe): "somewhere" isn't enough. Even if evil is everywhere, good is present too, and reflection on what we've just seen shows that a triply transcendent but non-ultimate reality needn't be responsible for both. Perhaps like Mill's deity, at least metaphorically, it is struggling for the good of the world. In that case it might be metaphysically transcendent, responsible for what goes on somewhere in nature, *precisely by being responsible for at least some of the good in nature.* Because of this problem, I'd suggest, at least a necessary condition for the success of an argument from evil in a context like ours is that its target be a claim about things ultimate.

So let's make the transition to ultimism. The critic who was assigned the task of producing a problem of evil will likely think that her job is now going to be a lot easier. Is she right?

Well, how might a problem of evil for ultimism be presented? Let's try an inconsistency argument again. The explanation of everything in the world must somehow go back to whatever is metaphysically ultimate. But then horrors—those most awful things that happen in the world, highlighted by the problem of evil—are explanatorily traceable to whatever is metaphysically ultimate. Now, surely it's obvious that we can always conceive a reality greater than one to which the existence of horrors is in any sense traceable—namely, one for which that is not the case! Hence whatever is metaphysically ultimate in the world cannot be the greatest conceivable reality; it cannot be *axiologically* ultimate. But ultimism says it is. So ultimism is false and should be disbelieved.

Does this argument work? I think the adherent of evolutionary religion would be right to be dubious. Here it's especially helpful to see the contrast with arguments from evil against traditional *theism*—the proposition usually attacked in this way. Ultimism is Thin/Strong whereas theism is Thick/Strong. So there's more to get hold of, as it were, when attacking theism; more conceptual space for your arrow to strike. We may, in particular, be able to see how a more loving or empathetic *person* than any to whom the existence of horrors is in any sense traceable could exist. By, as it were, giving to the Ultimate a face, and allowing what is already known about persons and love and personal relationship to be determinative of what would be the case if there were a Divine reality, we sharply restrict the relevant intellectual options in such a way that a skepticism-proof conclusion can arguably be drawn. Here we are, as it were, dealing with a religious idea at close range—it is familiarly personal and thus accessible to our reasoning.

But without being able to make use of specific insights about how loving or empathetic persons behave, I don't feel I know my way around sufficiently well to have any confidence at all in the critic's conclusion. When we take the artificial restrictions away, removing our traditional conceptions and working with ultimism instead of any more limited religious "ism"—then evolutionary skepticism once again looms. At our early stage of evolution, with the center of religion before our minds instead of some possibly misleading present interpretation thereof, we have to say that personality, at least as we know it, may not at all be part of the Ultimate, or may have a place in the Divine something like that of the single numeral "2" in a page of Einstein's equations. Similarly, we can't assume that the familiar axiological concepts from the personal realm, as negotiated thus far, tell the complete and final truth about value, but must rather acknowledge that the complete and final truth about value might still be quite beyond us.

Our objector, who thinks the problem of evil defeats ultimism, is forced to deny all this. In a much more general way than the traditional atheist, she is claiming that no matter *what* the final and complete parameters for an understanding of value may turn out to be, there is no way in which what is metaphysically ultimate could be axiologically ultimate if there are horrors. Here we should hesitate. Perhaps many of our thoughts about what really matters or about how value is realized in things are still very limited and quite imperfect in their apprehension of the truth, and are so in ways affecting what we should think about the objector's claim, if we are to think truly. This might seem a sneaky getaway were it not for the effects of temporal contextualization, which arguably must include precisely such thoughts.

Of course this doesn't mean that *nothing* can presently be known about value. Let's not make that mistake. Indeed, I believe we can make at least some intellectual progress even in religious matters on the basis of what we already know about goods and evils. I agree with the objector that some propositions in this neighborhood are obviously true and so escape the problem of Total Evidence. Most fundamentally, we certainly must regard horrors as intrinsically very bad. How could one avoid thinking this without forsaking all thought? (Here remember our way of responding to the global skeptic in Chapter 3.) In my view one may also, as suggested above, reasonably believe certain claims about horrors and love and empathy, using them to argue against traditional theism—seeing here the possibility of a critical "next step" in inquiry about things religious. But ultimism, which tells us only *that* a Divine reality exists and not *how*, is another matter.

Notice that this point is confirmed instead of countered when soteriological considerations are brought in. As primitive as we are, hardly knowing what we are or how the history of intelligent life in the universe will unfold (in the more than 99 percent of its total duration that may remain), how are we in a position to judge that there is no religiously usable sense in which reality will turn out to be on the side of life, even if the sense that theism gives this idea is irremediably problematic? Here we should find ourselves without belief either way because we don't have enough to go on, at least not yet. There are too many obstacles, too many unfinished discussions, between ourselves and the truth in such a case for us to be sure that the light of the truth is here able to reach us, undeflected. Simply by considering the path of evolution leading up to this point, leaving the future aside, it may already strike us that this is good advice. Colin McGinn, as we've seen, argues that because of the particular course evolution has taken in our case, our brains are not cut out for the solving of problems puzzled over by philosophers, such as the mind/body problem and the problem of free will. Certain fundamental matters about the character and criteria of value are lurking nearby, and arguably would be treated similarly. Now *add* the facts about the future I have been emphasizing—the epistemic consequences of temporal contextualization—and you will have abundant reason to distinguish among the relevant value claims in the way I am recommending.

Again, such reasoning as this would be less than impressive in a theistic context, arguably inapplicable given the specific avenues of argument available to the atheist, grounded in what we know about persons and in the specific judgments about value entailed by theism. But I suggest it is more impressive here, and indeed successful. If so, there is nothing in the problem of evil to stand in the way of evolutionary religion, even if the latter is fleshed out in the specific ultimistic way I have proposed.

IS THE AFTERLIFE EPISTEMICALLY IMPOSSIBLE?

Like many denizens of the twenty-first century, I find the claim that there is an afterlife open to serious question. Or, rather, I find the claim open to serious question when the idea of an afterlife is taken literally, as entailing that the consciousness of at least some human beings survives the death of their physical bodies. Let's take it that way here. Moreover, although afterlife belief is often portrayed as hugely attractive, I'm not sure I'm on that bandwagon. Without my wife, my family, my friends, my work...where would I be? The naturalistic strands of our culture have had enough of an influence on me that death being a complete end seems, well, natural. The idea ceased to cause any serious agitation long ago. Of course if the alternatives were death and no-death instead of death-plus-afterlife and death-without-afterlife, the choice would be clear. Like Woody

Allen, I do think it would be good if I could achieve immortality through not dying!

But whatever our views or inclinations on this matter, the claim central to any form of religiousness, as religiousness is here conceived, appears to entail that there is an afterlife. Or at least it does so when taken together with certain well known facts about lives cut short or full of horrors. How is a transcendent good available to such lives if they end at death? It seems it can't be. I urged a similar point in relation to ultimism in the last chapter. The suggestion we are now considering widens this argument to include any religious claim at all, reasoning that for some of us, a transcendent good is available only if there is an afterlife, and so any claim to the effect that there is a triply transcendent (and thus a soteriologically transcendent) reality that accepts this fact is committed to the afterlife. This means, of course, that any problem attaching to the afterlife claim is at the same time a problem for religion—including evolutionary religion. Now, to turn this into a reason to reject evolutionary religion, the objector needs to do more than show that we should all be in *doubt* about the afterlife claim, for the participant in evolutionary religion is in doubt already and has built this condition into the nature of her religiousness. What needs to be shown is that the claim should be *disbelieved*, because clearly false. How might such an argument proceed?

Quite straightforwardly, these days. Many philosophers and scientists believe that there is strong evidence for thinking that brain death is followed by what Wes Morriston, a philosopher at the University of Colorado (Boulder), appropriately calls a "permanent experiential blank," and rather little evidence for thinking that conscious life continues. Brain damage, Morriston reminds us, can profoundly alter a person's mind and personality. New capacities (for example, an appreciation for gourmet food or classical music) may be acquired; often old capacities are lost. Brain trauma can also render a person wholly unconscious. Facts like these are numerous and very well known. Taken together, they strongly suggest that one's conscious life depends on the functioning of one's brain. In the absence of evidence to the contrary, it is natural to conclude that the destruction of the brain brings with it the permanent cessation of consciousness.

Should we who know of these considerations be led by them into anti-afterlife belief? I've already said that serious questioning of afterlife belief seems warranted, but outright disbelief? Well, let's see what happens to the force of those considerations when we add to them what we've learned about our primitivity and the need for temporal contextualization. Recall the proposal from the end of Chapter 3 concerning a set of *six properties* a candidate belief might have: precision, detail, profundity, attractiveness, ambition, and controversiality. The proposal was that where all of these properties are present in a high degree, a diligent inquirer will be prevented by recognition of this fact from forming the belief. In such circumstances he will rightfully be led by recognition of our two-sided immaturity to instead be in doubt as to whether whatever evidence he has for the belief in question is representative of the Total Evidence. And where *most* of the properties are present, a belief is still made vulnerable and needs special life support to survive as a reasonable belief. How does the belief that there is no afterlife fare when we judge it by this standard?

Not very well. It is precise, having clear content, and also—contrary to what may at first seem the case—rather detailed, and so it has many alternatives; there are many ways in which it could be false. Why is it detailed? Well, consider the difference between this belief and another we might consider: that we do not live on due to the brain's being miraculously revivified, in every case, by God at exactly one second after complete brain death. This proposition specifies *one particular way* in which there could be an afterlife and says that *it* is not realized. The proposition has but one significant alternative, its denial (which says that the dead brain *is* thus revivified, every time), and our evidence for the falsehood of that alternative is about as strong as can be imagined. And we are safely led by this evidence into the belief that the form of afterlife in question is not realized, despite what our skeptical criterion has to say. For not only is the property of detail absent from the belief that that particular form of afterlife is not realized, but so are profundity, ambition, attractiveness, and controversiality (if you're wondering about profundity, notice that the proposition doesn't purport to express any deep and comprehensive understanding of the nature of things; it only rules out one way in which there could be an afterlife). Now let's bring back into this paragraph the belief that there is *no* afterlife. This belief, by contrast, rules out *every* way in which there could be an afterlife. It is in fact equivalent to a large conjunction of denials, corresponding to all the ways in which there could be an afterlife: it says there is no afterlife of this sort *and* no afterlife of that sort (and so on and so on). This makes it rather detailed. And this detail contributes to its evolutionary vulnerability because each form of afterlife mentioned represents an alternative to the anti-afterlife belief—a way it could be false.

So we have precision and detail in the anti-afterlife belief, and because of this, many alternatives. But we also have a certain degree of profundity: a fairly deep understanding of our nature and destiny comes with such a belief, and many other understandings are ruled out. For one thing, as the objector himself claims, if there is no afterlife at all, of any kind, then no religious understanding of the world can be on the right track. Notice that this means that every religious view is an alternative to the anti-afterlife claim! What follows is surely that there may well be many alternatives to the anti-afterlife belief we don't yet know. However large the conjunction of afterlife denials we can create, there may still be forms of afterlife we haven't thought of, perhaps tied to forms of transcendence we don't or can't know. We're ruling these out too when we say there is no afterlife. Are we really in a position to do so?

Next we have attractiveness, and this, you say, need not be worried about: no one finds the idea of there being no afterlife attractive. Indeed, quite the contrary! I see the point—though I think it can be overstated in a culture where naturalistic thinking is so influential. And I think that, by the same token, we also easily ignore some of the reasons for which an afterlife may be defended, especially in evolutionary religion. To put the point most pointedly: existentially weary, one might *relish* the idea of being completely extinguished and yet embrace the religious idea of an afterlife because of the deep justice—the opportunity for all to achieve their full potential—that must forever be given up if no such thing exists. The anti-afterlife belief, as this suggests, may come to have its own attractiveness.

However that may be, we don't need attractiveness in the anti-afterlife belief to help us generate skepticism about the afterlife because we have *ambition*—and we have it in spades. Of course we also have controversiality, but ambition is perhaps the property that's most important here. For the afterlife question is completely entangled in a set of knotted issues concerning the nature of consciousness and the nature of the self that, as we have seen, McGinn declares insoluble by the human mind given the way it has evolved. How do we know that there aren't positions we can't understand supported by evidence we couldn't assess which entail that there is an afterlife? How can we rule out the existence of facts—whether discoverable by us or not—that cancel the force of those physical facts on which arguments against the afterlife are based? Now, note carefully that I'm not saying it might be the case that mental events are *not* causally dependent on brain processes. I'm saying that even if this is indeed undeniably the case, it might, because of what the correct solutions to problems of consciousness and the self and religion contain, *also* be a fact that in one way or another *I* am not thus dependent, or that even if I am, a new "platform" for mental activity can be acquired.

So to complete our tally: of the properties mentioned by our criterion, the belief that there is no afterlife has five: precision, detail, profundity, ambition, and controversiality. This doesn't immediately indicate the reasonableness of skepticism, according to that standard, but it certainly does make for vulnerability in believing. And in my own view the detail of such a belief combined with the unusual depth of its ambition are alone sufficient to clinch the case for evolutionary skepticism. (Remember that there may, in this case or that, be "sufficient conditions" of skepticism other than the one I have particularly emphasized.)

Here's another way of putting my point, which links it more explicitly to the problem of Total Evidence. The objection we are considering spoke of there being strong evidence that there is no afterlife of any sort and *no evidence to the contrary*. But that is true only if what is meant is that we have no strong evidence to the contrary *at present*. And who knows what new evidence may emerge in the more than 99 percent of intelligent inquiry that may still lie ahead of us, especially in relation to a belief so detailed and ambitious? Drawing a conclusion now and forming disbelief in an afterlife would because of this rather large question mark be premature.

Precisely because of what we know about our ignorance concerning consciousness (presently a hugely controversial subject) and what we don't know about how deep that ignorance is (more generally, what we don't know concerning how ignorant we may be about our own nature and, not unrelatedly, about the ultimate structure of reality)—because of all this, denying the afterlife today instead of accepting skepticism on that vexed subject is more like denying that any model of string theory scientists will conceive can be made to work than it is like, say, denying a theory of evolution without natural selection. Now, if we had a clear picture of how the brain produces consciousness, assuming it does, or even a satisfying way of identifying what consciousness is, or if there were in this vicinity some apparently necessary truths to guide us, things might be different, but as things stand, skepticism is the order of the day.

It may be appropriate as we conclude this discussion of the anti-afterlife claim to return to an assumption obviously needed by the objector—that soteriological transcendence can't be had *without* an afterlife. At the beginning I said that this seems to be true, but it's worth considering what a skeptical approach, which we've applied to anti-afterlife belief, might have to say about this assumption. Given the deep issues about value and human nature lurking here, it too seems rather ambitious. Now, where ultimism—and thus ultimate well-being—are at issue, it may be hard indeed to see how one *could* have the soteriological element of religion, in all cases, without an afterlife. That's why I came to the view I did in the previous chapter. But it's not clear to me that this holds across the board, for just any feasible way in which evolutionary religion might come to be.

Take, for example, a form of evolutionary religion that goes Thin/Weak and, instead of taking on board the traditional afterlife claim, argues that soteriological transcendence might be realized variously. It proposes that even the following should be regarded as epistemically possible for us: the deepest and most poignant facts from everyone's Earthly existence—including that of those who suffer horrifically or die young—contribute in some way (though perhaps one undetectable by us) to a final unity of things, and will be known and fully appreciated with a depth of empathy we could never reach by some inconceivably evolved mind or minds in the deep future.

Is this epistemically possible? And, if so, do we have an alternative conception of an afterlife that is religiously usable? One with any soteriological bite? I myself am not left believing the right answer to be yes in each case. But I also don't believe that there isn't *some* such idea in conceptual space that *does* work—at any rate for a non-ultimistic form of evolutionary religion—and so I believe that such an idea is worth seeking. If it were found through religious inquiry, then there might be another way of showing that the anti-afterlife objection can be answered.

IS NONBELIEVING FAITH JUST WISHFUL THINKING?

Let's turn now to several rather different objections, which address not the truth of the claim central to evolutionary religion and what it entails, but rather the appropriateness or significance of the form of life developed in response to such claims. With the first I give voice to what may be an especially tempting charge: that nonbelieving religious faith, whether dressed up as a form of acceptance or assumption or trust or imagination, really comes down to a disagreeable sort of *wishful thinking*.

What exactly is wishful thinking, and what makes it disagreeable or objectionable? As usually intended, "wishful thinking" means wishful *believing*. It's the kind of thing that makes you think (read: believe) that you'll get that job you really want but are quite unqualified for. As this example suggests, the belief instantiated by wishful thinking may be yours thanks to self-deception. And it's not hard to see why a critic would find self-deception disagreeable! But is there self-deception in evolutionary religion? Has the one who practices nonbelieving faith deceived herself into believing there is a transcendent reality or that ultimism is true? Clearly not—this is a contradictory notion. Nonbelieving faith is, after all, *nonbelieving*. And if the objection here amounts to an unwillingness to accept that faith as I've described it really *is* nonbelieving, then I refer the objector back to arguments in Chapter 6—in particular, ones distinguishing between intellectual attitudes with reference to the extent to which they are voluntary. It is especially by being deeply voluntary, both in their inception and as maintained over time, that the attitudes I have recommended for the faith of the future display their nonbelieving status.

But there are still a couple of ways in which we might try to link wishful thinking, self-deception, and faith more convincingly. First, it might be suggested that the one who practices nonbelieving faith has, because of what she wishes were true, deceived herself into believing that the religious claim in question *is epistemically possible instead of false*. Really, it's false. If the religious person saw things clearly she would be disbelieving that claim instead of embracing it in nonbelieving faith. Or, second, it may be suggested that nonbelieving faith will over time *turn into* religious belief—with the first stage just a way of getting to the second, which one really wants—through slow self-deception.

The first claim here is just that: a claim. It needs an argument to back it up that will *show* that no religious claim is epistemically possible. Now, we've already looked at the two main ways of trying to provide such an argument, the problem of evil and the anti-afterlife argument, finding both unsuccessful. So the claim in question may be set aside. As for the second new way of linking wishful thinking, self-deception, and faith: the adherent of evolutionary religion sees that religious belief is just wrong for primitives like us—indeed, this is part of what defines her stance. So she does not find religious belief desirable and isn't motivated to use nonbelieving faith as a way to get to religious belief. Quite the contrary. What this second objection is not yet taking seriously is the idea that in evolutionary religion it's not business as usual, religiously. The temporalist perspective provides a whole new way of approaching religion, in which the attitude of religious believing is seen as a problem rather than a solution. Anyone who signs up for evolutionary religion is taking on that perspective, and should be regarded accordingly.

Let's now consider two other ways of trying to give life to the wishful thinking objection, which don't rely on claims about self-deception. One has it that nonbelieving faith means getting lost in pleasant reveries over things that might well be false and, in that absorbed state, missing—or giving less than due attention to—things that are true. The other has a problem with the fact that by adopting nonbelieving faith one is using *intellectual* attitudes to pursue *non-truth-oriented desires*. Even in an evolutionary context—indeed, especially there, given the need to discipline our wayward thoughts and grow into maturity—we should want our intellectual attitudes, whether nonbelieving or believing, to reflect only a pursuit of truth, and should want to respond positively to no proposition that the available evidence doesn't strongly support. Any other attitude, this objection says, is beneath the dignity of the most admirable sort of twenty-first century intellectual.

Is either of these two ways of reasoning any better than its unsuccessful siblings? Better perhaps, but still unsuccessful. Take the first of the two. When one concentrates on something desirable that might be true but also might be false, one needn't neglect the facts. Consider a nonreligious example. You're lost in the woods and having a hard time keeping it together, mentally. You might get out, and then again you might not. Of course you really want to. When you decide to have faith that you'll get out even though you don't believe it, are you becoming absorbed with something desirable in such a way that you'll be led to miss important facts? It's hard to see why you should be. Indeed, having got it together, you may now see things more clearly! What's more, it's because of your sensitivity to the full range of relevant facts, which included your nearly unmanageable anxiety, that you decided to have faith in the first place. And if there's new evidence of being irretrievably lost that, because of your faith, takes a bit longer to get through to you, is this information that you *should* have been aware of? That could be true only if you shouldn't have faith, and we've already seen how faith may be justified in this case. Moreover, in the calmed condition of faith, you're more likely to pick up on epistemic facts in *favor* of your survival, should they arise, than you'd otherwise be.

So things are a lot more complicated here than the objector allows, and some of these complications remove the force of the objection, at least in nonreligious contexts. In the next chapter we'll see how things are rather similar religiously. So stay tuned.

The points just raised also suggest a way to respond to the second of the new and improved wishful thinking objections: faith can serve non-intellectual and intellectual purposes at the same time. But let's consider that objection a bit more fully. Recall that it says it's wrong to use intellectual attitudes in the pursuit of non-truth-oriented desires. Is this true?

Actually, no. Despite their name, not all intellectual attitudes *need* be directed to truth either directly or indirectly to be justified. Certainly this is the case in nonreligious contexts. So long as one allows—as presumably, to avoid undue narrowness, the critic would—that non-truth-oriented desires (say, wanting one's political party to win or wanting war to cease) are not simply off limits for our intellectual, and so long as it can reasonably be thought that non-believing faith is sometimes the best way to pursue such a desire, even the admired intellectual may, without losing any tincture of admirableness, employ it to do so. The latter condition—that non-believing faith reasonably be thought the best way to pursue such a desire—is often satisfied: consider again the case where you're lost in the woods and imaginative faith (or some sort of nonbelieving faith) that you'll get out is critical to keeping it together. And, as we'll see, it's satisfied religiously too. It would be unduly rigid to say that nonbelieving faith is unreasonable in such circumstances—and this even if it's *entirely* non-truth-oriented.

Now, what we *can* say is that, other things being equal, you shouldn't use intellectual attitudes for non-intellectual ends if this will in some way *interfere* with a proper and morally admirable pursuit of truth and understanding. This seems quite reasonable. But should we expect such interference in the context of evolutionary religion? Pretty clearly no. After all, it's only after careful investigation leads someone to skepticism that, in my depiction of imaginative religion, the commitment to imagine the world religiously begins. And in imagining that some religious claim (perhaps ultimism) is true, our skeptic imagines not that the *available* evidence is any different than it is, which would indeed be unreasonable, but rather that the Total Evidence, about which no belief is at present justified, speaks in favor of that claim. Since this may well be the case, the adherent of evolutionary religion is not directing her mind in any way that she sees or should see may well lead her astray. Nothing known or reasonably believed to be false is here imagined as true. Furthermore, she can make the imaginative commitment in response to *arguments* supporting it—again, stay tuned—and so from the side of reason, not from the side of an unreflective and traditional religious sensibility.

In his brief comments on the imagination, mentioned in the last chapter, John Stuart Mill agrees that imaginative faith (he says hope) is unreasonable if imaginatively dwelling on evidentially unproven ideas disturbs "the rectitude of the intellect and the right direction of the actions and will." But, as he too points out, this need not be the case. In support of his view Mill offers the example of a "cheerful disposition." This, he says, is "always accounted one of the chief blessings of life" and yet what is it "but the tendency, either from constitution or habit, to dwell chiefly on the brighter side of the present and of the future?" He elaborates: "If every aspect, whether agreeable or odious of every thing, ought to occupy exactly the same place in our imagination which it fills in fact, and therefore ought to fill in our deliberate reason, what we call a cheerful disposition would be but one of the forms of folly." So is cheerfulness folly? No, says Mill, cheerful people are no less alive to the dangers and other challenges of life, including intellectual ones, and indeed are better prepared to meet them because "a hopeful disposition gives a spur to the faculties and keeps all the active energies in good working order."

Perhaps evolutionary religion will turn out to be something like a cheerful disposition. In any case, I suspect we've seen enough to avoid being prevented by the wishful thinking objection from giving careful consideration to arguments for evolutionary religion.

GUILT BY ASSOCIATION WITH NEW
AGE RELIGION?

Wishful thinking is not the only charge a critic of evolutionary faith will find tempting. Some comments of mine about skeptical-imaginative ultimistic faith that appeared in a recent essay online were tartly dismissed by a Christian commentator familiar with my rejection of traditional theism in the following terms: "The fuzziness of these New-Age-sounding attitudes is enough to make one nostalgic for that old-time atheism of J. L. Mackie and Antony Flew." I found the comparison with "new age" religion—and also the suggestion that atheists ought uncreatively to stay in old familiar places—amusing. But then I had a more serious thought. My conservative critic had done me a service: he helped me to see that in exploring the possibility of a "new time" religion which even openminded atheists should find interesting, I also need to preempt any conflating of what I am up to with what is intellectually objectionable in so-called new age religion.

It shouldn't be hard to make this distinction. For one thing, new age religion, insofar as it is intellectually objectionable (and there's no reason to suppose that all of it must be), features a careless syncretism or mixing of detailed religious ideas. This is what the oft-mentioned "fuzziness" consists in. But ultimistic faith, and indeed any "thin" faith of the sort likely to appeal to the evolutionarily minded, excludes such details. What my conservative critic saw as fuzziness is in fact a *lack* of detail, not mixed-up details. Maybe he was assuming that every religious vision must bristle with interlocked details, and not being able to make out mine, concluded that they are fuzzy. That assumption would be an example of an error I have been trying to root out.

Objectionable new age religion also features a strong and virtually immoveable belief that the spiritual realm is real. This too is absent from any nonbelieving faith response, which presupposes skepticism. New age belief, moreover, may arise and flourish within a perspective naively ignorant of science, and sometimes flies in the face of established scientific results. Evolutionary religion, on the other hand, grows in part from respect for the results of science; its skepticism is an evolutionary skepticism and it boasts no specific results of the sort that could possibly come in conflict with established science.

Finally, it is often complained that new age religion is rootless and superficial (this is related to the "fuzziness" point), forgoing the riches of a long tradition for swiftly shifting infatuations of the moment. Here there might seem to be more of a connection with evolutionary religion, since the latter too can appear relatively unconcerned about the past. But what the religious perspective I have described proposes for us, though in a sense new, is a demanding commitment instead of some brief dalliance. And it is deeply rooted in a serious evolutionary perspective, which can absorb the fullest, most finegrained understanding of the history of religion (and indeed is in part based on it). Moreover, it can, as we saw in the last chapter, learn from past religiousness without becoming defined by it.

So evolutionary religion is not to be confused with new age religion. In particular, there is no spiritual interest here that grows from confusion or religious illiteracy and that could just as well or better be sated by getting fully acquainted with the heart of some tradition such as Christianity. Rather we have a monumental shift from past to future within an evolutionary skepticism that places *all* existing religious claims in doubt—so-called new age as much as traditional. We must never forget the broad background to our discussion, developed in the first half of the book. It is against this evolutionary backdrop that we are coming to grips with the adventurous question whether a new and better start for religion might be possible.

HOW COULD SUCH A THING EVER CATCH ON?

But how satisfyingly adventurous can discussion of this question really be if the possibility I'm proposing is never going to catch on? If evolutionary religion were a new age phenomenon it might at least be expected to have some appeal in contemporary culture! But as it is—so goes our next and last objection—that is not the case. Any religious form of life focused on a *thin* religious concept (whether ultimism or some other) is going to find itself at a disadvantage, when it enters the religious marketplace, next to traditional forms of religion whose ideas are full of exciting details. As the cognitive science of religion (CSR) is starting to reveal, religion thrives on minimally-counterintuitive (MCI) concepts, which can at bottom be ordinary, even mundane, concepts, but have an important ontological twist.

Take, for example, the ordinary concept of a person. Now add the twist that you get with the concept of a *superhuman* person. Such concepts are particularly attention-grabbing—they are memorable and do well religiously: consider only how the notion of a super-human person has caught on and allowed theism to flourish. Indeed, there is growing evidence from CSR that humans generally use cognitive mechanisms that favor agent-centered religious ideas. But no thin religious concept, so it will be said, is an MCI or agent-centered concept, and so people are likely to be left cold by such a concept. Perhaps we need another pair of conceptual options to add to those of the previous chapter: Cold/Warm. A thin concept is cold. Thus even if I can defend my religious skepticism, my proposals about evolutionary religion will never catch on.

Perhaps the most obvious thing to say to this objection is that evolutionary religion should not be expected to appeal to everyone, but only to those who have followed the path through evolutionary skepticism and come out on the other side. (This is not elitism, just a factual point about who will perceive its relevance. Besides, my arguments make evolutionary skepticism available to virtually every-one.) In particular, I expect it may appeal to those whom we might call "twenty-first century evolutionary skeptics"—people who realize that this is *only* the twenty-first century, and are sensitive to what I have called the Great Disparity between the few thousand years of thought and feeling we've invested in religion so far and the possibil-ity of millions to come (if not for us, then for species that follow us). Now, clearly, such religious skepticism is a relevant cultural phenom-enon. Thus any religious view compatible with it and engaging it would have to be regarded as culturally relevant, too. And who knows what might grow from this beginning?

Furthermore, even within an evolutionary religious commitment, personal and agential notions need not entirely disappear. Even an atheist—and not all advocates of evolutionary religion will be atheists, denying traditional theism; some will be agnostics instead—is only committed to the notion that the Ultimate, if it exists, is not *exclu-sively* or *fundamentally* a personal reality (where the meaning of "personal" can be reached by extrapolation from our present selves). It's quite compatible with this that personal qualities, or something like personal qualities, should still appear and play some role in the nature of the Divine, where they are joined to other features of ultimacy we cannot presently or perhaps ever conceive (maybe even ones to which, collectively, some possible descendant of our "person" concept would apply, though we may never evolve in such a way as to be able to see it). Hence, although a nonbelieving commitment to a proposition like ultimism does not entail a commitment to personal religious ideas, it retains, at various levels, a degree of openness to them, and this even for traditional atheists.

And how about this? Could an MCI concept from one time function as the ordinary concept of a later time, and at that later time provide the base for another, higher-level MCI shift? We're familiar with dead metaphors, which are certainly less attention-grabbing than live ones. Well, maybe something analogous can happen with MCI concepts, when their familiarity makes them ordinary. You can probably see where I'm going with this. *Traditional theism is becoming ordinary.* Maybe in cultural conditions like ours there is the possibility of a higher-level MCI shift to something like ultimism.

Indulge me and assume, just for the sake of discussion, that evolutionary thinking, including a keen awareness of the Great Disparity and the imperative of temporal contextualization, spreads through most of humanity within the next two hundred years. Suppose as well that knowledge of the rich diversity of religious thinking from around the world continues to grow and spread. The former development would of course make skepticism about religion more difficult to resist. The latter, together with the former, would make thin concepts like ultimism (properly understood) more widely attractive: they offer a mosaic of possibilities to tantalize and enrich the imagination within a general core affirmation, recognized as more appropriate to an early stage of evolution than any *detailed* core affirmation at *war* with others. This idea is only one or two ontological twists past theism: we're talking about a Divine reality that is not exclusively personal but may contain personal elements within it, alongside perhaps infinitely many others within a rich metaphysical medley, much of it wholly mysterious to us now, of the sort that we might expect to find realized in a truly ultimate and unlimitedly rich reality. The point is that evolutionary religion might easily become *more* attention-grabbing within a cultural context like ours.

Interesting empirical support for this judgment comes from religious surveys showing the rise of what are often called the "nones": persons who have no religious affiliation. Perhaps surprisingly, these individuals are not predominantly secular. The story is more complex, suggesting that religion may be changing rather than going away.

For example, in a 2008 report called *American Nones: The Profile of the No Religion Population* released by the respected ARIS (American Religious Identification Survey), one reads that "the Nones increased from 8.1 percent of the U.S. adult population in 1990 to 15 percent in 2008 and from 14 to 34 million adults. Their numbers far exceed the combined total of all the non-Christian religious groups in the U.S." Furthermore: "whereas Nones are presently 15 percent of the total adult U.S. population, 22 percent of Americans aged 18–29 years self-identify as Nones. Regarding belief in the divine, most Nones are neither atheists nor theists but rather agnostics and deists (59 percent) and perhaps best described as skeptics." There is also this tidbit: "Nones are much more likely to believe in human evolution (61 percent) than the general American public (38 percent)." Then we have an intriguing contrast with the new age movement and another reference to skepticism: an "incorrect assumption is that large proportions of Nones are anti-rationalist proponents of New Age and supernatural ideas. . . . [T]hey are more likely to be rational skeptics." The report concludes with these words: "In the future we can expect more American Nones given that 22 percent of the youngest cohort of adults self-identify as Nones and they will become tomorrow's parents. If current trends continue and cohorts of non-religious young people replace older religious people, the likely outcome is that in two decades the Nones could account for around one-quarter of the American population."

Little can be inferred, perhaps, from these facts about recent changes in American culture. But they will appear tantalizing for anyone interested in the prospects for evolutionary religion. In the context of the other arguments whose force we've noted, they suggest that a convincing case for the idea that evolutionary religion will never catch on has not been made.

8

Religion for Pioneers

> We are just at the beginning of a new age of religious searching, whose outcome no one can foresee.
>
> Charles Taylor, *A Secular Age*

I'm a Canadian, but when I was a boy I loved stories of the American frontier. I talked about it too. Maybe a bit too much: in school my nicknames ranged from Black Hawk to Daniel Boone, and I wasn't always being complimented. A bookish kid, I wanted to find out *what really happened*—in history, especially among the pioneers—and then I couldn't help letting other people know. I ordered the most authoritative biography of Boone then available from New Jersey and, having read it, pointed out mistakes in the World Book Encyclopedia to the town librarian. "Daniel Boone never really wore a coonskin cap!" That sort of thing. On the single occasion when they agreed to watch it with me, I pointed out some obvious errors in the popular TV show *Daniel Boone* to a couple of my friends. "Look, here they've got a young Boone still in Kentucky meeting Lincoln's parents, who are about to have a baby, which means this is 1809 [the year of Lincoln's birth], a time when Boone was in fact already living in Missouri and 75! Can you believe it?!"

As I grew, it became clear that, since the American frontier was indeed history, I'd have to find a new frontier to explore. Eventually I discovered philosophy. Here were people using nothing but their bare reason in an assault on some really big questions, to figure out *what really is true*. I was hooked. I still am. But I sometimes wonder whether a bit of that old pioneering interest survived the transition to my new calling. I glimpse it from time to time in the directions my philosophical work has taken—especially lately. For there is certainly a sense in which my perspective on deep time allows us be pioneers. Intellectual pioneers, certainly, but spiritual ones too.

Of course that deep time perspective, which includes our incredibly early position in the possible history of intelligent life on our planet, is not just mine. It is the perspective of science, as we saw in this book's first pair of chapters. That scientific perspective has skeptical consequences epistemologically, as we saw in the second pair—ones that undermine both religious and irreligious belief. But instead of standing around wondering what to do, we need to see how this skepticism, because of the unique *kind* of skepticism it is, has opened up a brand new possibility for religion even as it takes some old ones away. How a skeptical religiousness shaped by evolutionary ideas might come to be was explored in the book's third pair of chapters.

Now we have come to the last chapter of the book, the second of its final pair, focused on the defense of that new religious possibility— the defense of evolutionary religion. We've already seen, in the previous chapter, how some basic objections to evolutionary religious practice, whether as I've proposed we conceive it or without that particular imprint, can be answered. So we've cleared them away. They won't be obscuring the view. But the view of what? What, if anything, can be put in their place as a more positive reason or set of reasons—reasons for thinking not just that evolutionary religion isn't clearly wrongheaded, undesirable, or unworthy, but that such religiousness is fully appropriate to our place in evolutionary time? How, if at all, can we move from an assessment of "if anyone did this sort of thing we shouldn't particularly mind" to one of "this ought to be encouraged: it's desirable or admirable given the distinctive features of our temporal position"? Several times I've spoken of the goal as discovery of a form of religion appropriate to our time—one that *fits* us. To complete our task as intellectual and spiritual pioneers, to suggest a full solution to the problems of religion in our culture, we need to see whether evolutionary religion can fully live up to that description.

I have some arguments that just may do the job. They first emerged when I realized that it might be worth exploring one last reversal or turnaround in our ways of thinking. We've already seen the need to turn from the past to the full expanse of deep time, both past and future; from theism and other detailed religious "isms" to something more general like ultimism; and from belief to imaginative faith. The final reversal I'm going to recommend concerns the view most philosophers take on the traditional arguments for belief in God, a rather negative one. Perhaps those arguments—ontological, cosmological, and so on—are not just failed attempts to buttress theistic belief. Perhaps they can function as starting points for *new* reasoning that will support evolutionary religion.

It can of course be tempting for an atheist like me to take the usual unqualifiedly negative line about theistic arguments. But I found myself asking: What if they're simply misdirected? What if, in a moment of intellectual evolution, those old arguments or the considerations inspiring them can be recast—adapted—as arguments for another religious conclusion: that evolutionary religion fits our present stage of development in the fullest sense?

After experimenting with the idea, it seems to me to be rather promising—though of course I'm also interested in what forms of support for evolutionary religion will seem promising to other minds. In this chapter I want to share some of the results of this experimentation. To make the experiments work, we need to activate the idea of *aims that we primitives should find appealing, precisely because we are primitives*. In each case, some fiddling with the ideas animating the thinking of some classical figure—Anselm of Canterbury, Gottfried Wilhelm Leibniz, William Paley, and William James are our four—allows a reason to emerge for supposing that some such aim is best pursued within the context of evolutionary religion. To instead, in a nonbelieving way, accept metaphysical naturalism or remain in an uncommitted skepticism will tend to mean—even if there are exceptions—that it's harder to achieve these aims.

If this can be shown, we will have a pragmatic and evolutionary rationale for nonbelieving religious faith, and so the fourth and last condition of evolutionary religion set out in Chapter 5, religious pragmatism, will have proved to be satisfiable. Traditional religion might have *inhibited* evolutionary development (and might even inhibit acceptance of the idea of evolution), but the new evolutionary religion, touched by temporal contextualization, can be a vehicle of highly positive cultural evolution, a straight and narrow path leading us through the challenges of tomorrow.

This, at any rate, is what I will now argue. Be prepared to hear more about pioneering as I do.

ANSELM'S IDEA

The medieval Christian thinker Anselm of Canterbury had a big idea: the idea of something-than-which-a-greater-cannot-be-thought. Though this idea is usually taken—and may have been taken by him—to entail the idea of a person-like God, it does no such thing: it is far closer to the general idea of ultimism than to theism. In his famous work, the *Proslogion*, Anselm claims that he can prove from this idea alone that there must be something corresponding to it. The fool has said in his heart that there is no God, we read in the Psalms, and he really must be a fool, we read in Anselm's *Proslogion*. For if something-than-which-a-greater-cannot-be-thought does not exist, then it isn't really something-than-which-a-greater-cannot-be-thought. After all, then it could be greater! This is a condensed version of the familiar *Ontological Argument for the Existence of God*: that name appears, just so, in hundreds of textbooks reciting Anselm's words, usually without any indication that it is Immanuel Kant's name for the argument, affixed some seven centuries after Anselm expired, rather than Anselm's own.

Anselm's argument, as all atheists (and many theists too, including Kant) inform us, is unsuccessful. It too has expired: look closely, and you will see through the magic. Of course some theists resist. Even the great twentieth-century mathematician Kurt Gödel thought he might have a way of making the argument work. But let's suppose the critics are right. Suppose that hidden inside each member of the ontological family of arguments is a verbal trick or logical error of some kind. And then let's turn our heads to one side and look at everything animating Anselm from a somewhat different angle.

Reading his work again, we may notice that, more than a logical trickster, he spoke out of deep feeling for the greatness of something-than-which-a-greater-cannot-be-thought—feeling that made this new argument of his, an argument of a heady ontological sort, appear no more than appropriate. He had dimly sensed the argument's presence for some time and struggled to spell it out. And then one day while in a religious service: "Of course! That's obviously how things must be! How could I have been fool enough to have missed it!" And even if we sadly think that logic does not agree, we *may* agree with this much: that there is something grand about Anselm's struggle with something-than-which-a-greater-cannot-be-thought. We can see that Anselm's own mind is expanded by seeking to hold the Big

Idea. And, by meditating on this fact even after concluding that the original pattern of ontological reasoning is a failure, we can, I suggest, discover a *new* way of reasoning that shows how the practice of evolutionary religion is both desirable *and* admirable. Anselm, by getting us to think about his idea, to spend time with it, still speaks to us today—and especially today, given the early stage of religious development we are presently in.

For we too can be perplexed and frustrated and fascinated by his idea, when we come to hear of it. If we were less or differently evolved, we might never give it a thought. But now—there it is. What should we do with it? If we had already evolved to a more advanced state and could see that the Big Idea was unrealized, or else could really prove it to be realized (as the original Anselm thought he had), we would sadly disbelieve or else gladly believe. But, as things stand, all we can say for certain is that the claim that there is such a thing *might* be true—we are too immature, evolutionarily, to be in a position to rule its truth either out or in decisively. So what should we do in these circumstances? Just ignore the Idea? That doesn't seem right. It feels like an insult to the imagination. Let it play at the periphery of our minds? Allow it within range from time to time, here or there?

We now have another option. Having become temporally context-ualized, we can make a connection between such experiences as I've just described and evolutionary religion. Here we have the possibility of a deeper and more consistent engagement with the Idea in a sort of religious practice *without* belief. Let's think for a bit, within an Anselmian frame of reference, about why one might choose to practice religion in this way.

The Enlargement Aim

What may occur to us is that precisely as small-minded creatures, painfully aware of our multifaceted immaturity, it is good and fitting for us to always be on the lookout for new ways to expand and enrich and deepen and strengthen our minds. All of us have some intellectual pioneering to do. Call the aim referred to and recommended here the Enlargement Aim. We want to enlarge *ourselves*—deepening our capacities by pushing toward the big, not the little. And this is of course a goal we will set before ourselves not just individually but as a culture, insofar as temporal contextualization takes hold. Successfully pursuing this aim would be valuable in itself—quite respect-worthy and admirable. But it would also allow us more realistically to reach for greater attainments in the world, and so achieving this aim, whether alone or together with others, is highly *desirable* too. Evolutionary religion offers itself to us as the natural home for all such efforts and attainments.

Through the practice of evolutionary religion, especially if it receives an ultimistic cast, humans could make a *habit* of pushing thought and feeling to their very limits, savoring the notion of something unsurpassable in both reality and value in as many of its varied hues as the duration of life and the ingenuity of mind and heart permit. Naturalism, whether believed or accepted, and a skepticism unmixed with faith must here hold back, but evolutionary religion unbridles the imagination. And as a *religious* practice, it allows the Big Idea to provide the framework for all our doings. Thus evolutionary religion is an excellent way, arguably the best way (if only because it can enfold and inspire so many others), of pursuing the Enlargement Aim.

Evolutionary religion is especially able to prompt the capacities of the mind to grow because it commends a faith *without details*. Even Anselm was quick to fill out his Big Idea with details—Christian details. Such an act can relieve the immature mind of its duty to explore all possibilities, even those that are unconventional and seemingly strange, giving minute attention to everything the world might teach it about ultimate things. But just this duty can be made central to evolutionary religion. Certainly all three dimensions of nonbelieving faith as I developed the idea in Chapter 6—downward, inward, outward—challenge us continually to push and expand and deepen ourselves with the Ultimate as our imaginative reference point. Doing so will add to the texture and richness of our lives, and help us grow toward the greater maturity that religion-as-it-is often sadly inhibits. Evolutionary religion, we can therefore say, is good and reasonably pursued by creatures like us. It *fits* us, whatever might be said of other species of religion, because it encourages the fuller development of desirable human capacities and realizes intrinsically valuable states of mind: states of mind "mimicking" in some small way the qualities of their object. It facilitates pursuit of the Enlargement Aim. If fully engaged in, it might permit ever deeper and richer and more subtle expressions of our humanity to see the light of day.

Thus even if Anselm was mistaken and we aren't forced by logic to say that something-than-which-a-greater-cannot-be-thought exists, we do still get an argument for *treating* his Big Idea as realized in order to create a situation in which *we humans* can become greater than we are. Since this is an aim that is highly suited to primitives like us, regardless of what our other legitimate pursuits may be, it follows that evolutionary religion is highly appropriate to our place in time.

LEIBNIZ'S AMBITION

A few hundred years after Anselm, in the seventeenth century, we encounter another genius, the mathematician and philosopher Gottfried Leibniz, who had some interesting ideas of his own.

Leibniz is known for—among many other things—his invention of the infinitesimal calculus. Newton invented it independently around the same time, and the two thinkers and their disciples had a long-running dispute over priority. As this already suggests, Leibniz was a hugely ambitious man, and nowhere is his ambition more evident or deeper than in his graceful version of what in the textbooks (usually right after a discussion of Anselm) is called the *Cosmological Argument for the Existence of God.*

This argument is supposed to enable Leibniz to explain literally everything and thus lead him to the best of all possible consummations for human inquiry. Unfortunately, while as in all these cases discussion of the argument still continues, there is no agreement that Leibniz managed to pull off this feat. If you accept his "principle of sufficient reason" and define the universe as the total collection of contingent things (things that might not have existed), you will conclude, as Leibniz did, that the universe needs an explanation—a "sufficient reason" for its existence—and so something *non*-contingent (or necessarily existing) must exist independently of it. But it's not at all clear that reality satisfies Leibnizian preferences. Many fail to find Leibniz's principle rationally intuitive, and there's certainly no inductive generalization that will support it adequately on the basis of our explanatory experiences so far!

Suppose, however, that we stopped thinking about the cosmological argument of Leibniz and other arguments in the same family, considering instead how such argumentation—or considerations inspiring it—might be adapted to the needs of evolutionary religion. What might we find?

The Aim of Understanding

Leibniz's ambition, broadly conceived, was to promote intellectual understanding in the best possible way. And even if we can't argue that the best, most thorough, and of course true understanding of things will be religious—we're evolutionary skeptics, after all—we can still argue that the Leibnizian aim, which I will call the Aim of Understanding, is one that at our stage of development we are well advised to pursue, and that the best context for pursuing it is a religious context: namely, the one that evolutionary religion represents. It would certainly be ironic if such an argument could be made out successfully, given the number of times that religion's critics, looking backward only, have advanced the idea that religion undermines true inquiry and the unfettered pursuit of understanding. Perhaps faith can evolve so as to be *for* reason in a uniquely powerful way.

Let's consider how this ambition might be fulfilled through evolutionary religion. Three basic points suggest themselves: (i) evolutionary religion can provide additional *motivation* for early-stage intelligent creatures to pursue understanding; (ii) it can allow the predominantly secular investigative concerns of the twenty-first century to be *balanced* by a proper sort of religious investigation that, due to our immaturity, was neglected before; and (iii) it offers an effective way of pursuing the most comprehensive *unification* of understandings, something that has eluded us thus far but that on account of the brevity of our efforts shouldn't be given up—the richest possible overall understanding, in which fact and value are satisfyingly united. Motivation, balance, unification. We can see each to be highly desirable for creatures like us, and of course various admirable qualities belonging to intellectual virtue may come with them. I'll say a bit more about each in turn.

Additional motivation for inquiry of just any sort at all comes precisely from our immaturity conjoined with the nature of evolutionary religious activity as I have described it in Chapters 5 and 6. Since those who engage in such activity are skeptics, and since signs of the transcendent or the Ultimate can appear anywhere, the most scrupulous and open and wide-ranging investigative attitude must be cultivated by individuals and communities pursuing evolutionary religiousness. Here curiosity is excited instead of extinguished, and in a way that skepticism unmotivated by religion could hardly be expected to match consistently. True, all such inquiry goes on within a religious frame of reference and is integrated thereby—that's what makes it religious. But a religious focus like this doesn't imply that, say, your work on physics is going to have religious ideas imported into it; only that one of your reasons for doing physics will be the more general religious commitment.

A separate point can also be made here. For if investigation is built into religion, then there is another way for people to be drawn into it: not just additional but *crucial* motivation for inquiry might for some be provided, in a new dispensation, because they participate in evolutionary religion. There may be many who would not pursue inquiry much at all who now do so, insofar as evolutionary religion starts to make inroads culturally.

The "balance" point can be seen if we consider how little attention, in our short tenure on the planet, has been given to an open and wide-ranging exploration of alternative religious ideas—that is, to the exposure and discussion, from the perspective of a pure desire for understanding, of many alternative forms of transcendent and ultimistic ideas, both old and new. We are still at a pioneering stage here. For the last few centuries, because of the sudden rise in influence of modern science, naturalistic approaches have been in the ascendant and much careful attention has been devoted to their development; and before that rather limited and parochial religious options, many of them not developed in any credible or creditable intellectual manner, held sway. So a new program of research into religious options is needed to rectify the undesirable imbalance that we have now. This the acceptance of naturalism must impede, whereas evolutionary religion is ideally suited to facilitating it. And due to the sorts of impulse that give life to such religion, it can do so without the narrowing and stifling of creativity that has brought much past religion into intellectual disrepute.

Finally, if like Leibniz we want to further the *most comprehensive* possible understanding, there is a need to explore how science can be brought into harmony with what we sense from experience but still do not fully understand about such things as consciousness, value, and will. Especially given our immaturity as a species and the early stage of investigation we presently are in, we should not settle for truncated understandings which simply carve away what science seems to have a difficult time handling. Colin McGinn's arguments are again relevant: how do we know that the intellectual capacities we have, or have spent most time cultivating, are ones that will bring the desired insights? Of course we should remain open to science discovering, in time, how to handle all these things well enough on its own, and also to the appearance of clear evidence that such things *should* be dropped from our culture's intellectual agenda. (Naturalists, prematurely, hold that one or other of these things has happened already.) But if we love understanding, we might see the point of encouraging the ideas of evolutionary religion, which greatly broaden our frame of reference, and of acting on a newly evolved nonbelieving faith that what appears the richest possible understanding, in which fact and value most robustly construed are united, is in fact true. Perhaps only straining over long periods of time to see how the various discordant elements of our experience might be brought into harmony under such a conception will allow a fuller intellectual vision to be realized. Evolutionary religion has not only the requisite framework ideas but also offers the extra sources of inner fortitude that may be needed to keep the human research program going over the long haul. These are all *investigation*-oriented reasons for anyone who loves understanding and is deeply committed to its goals to promote the spread of evolutionary religion at this early stage of human existence. Thus Leibniz too, though in a certain sense he has been humbled, still speaks to us today, with his ambition for Understanding offering vital support to religion's cause.

PALEY'S WONDER

With William Paley we come to the last of the Big Three theistic "proofs" regularly recorded in traditional textbooks: the famous *Teleological Argument for the Existence of God*. Paley's argument for Divine design—for that is what it is, an attempt to show an intelligent design in nature (the Greek *telos* means "goal")—was read by Darwin long before he hit on the mechanism in nature, natural selection, that was to put Paley's painstaking designer of creaturely features out of a job. Darwinians often admire Paley's reasoning for its attempt at thoroughness and its author's honest exuberance over the wonders of nature. Richard Dawkins has expressed a certain affection for Paley, evidently regarding Paley as doing the best job of providing an explanation possible in his time and as sharing his own awe at the beautiful intricacies of the natural order. Of course these positive feelings coexist with a conviction that Paley's design argumentation is quite unsucc-essful! And latter day examples of design argumentation are likewise regarded as unsuccessful by most thinkers today.

Suppose this verdict is right. Can we turn positive feelings about Paley's wondering attitude toward the beautiful structures of nature into a different sort of reasoning—one that will strengthen evolution-ary religion even further?

The Aim of Respect for Beauty

I suggest we can. For by adopting evolutionary religion we are provided with a powerful way of pursuing several things which together should mark an important *telos* or goal for current human efforts at self-design through culture. I call it the Aim of Respect for Beauty: the aim (i) to honor the world's amazing and intricate beauty; (ii) to do justice to our most intense beauty-inspired experiences; (iii) to extend our appreciation of the world's beauty; and, not least, (iv) to contribute to the *preservation* of the world's beauty and of all the valuable and vulnerable forms of life that depend on the structures of nature we find beautiful. These goals are of course interconnected, and that is why I have gathered them all under a single Aim.

Like Paley and Darwin and Dawkins and many others, I have often wondered at the beauty of the world. It takes many forms. And all can tug at the mind to find some appropriate response—one truly worthy of such beauty. Trekking through a wet and darkly forested valley one cloudy day, I observed the sun freeing itself from the clouds and suddenly lighting up the hillsides. For a moment it seemed that everything was bathed in light: the experience of beauty was so powerful that it seemed unimaginable that there should be anything else. It lasted only for a few moments, and then I was returned to the "real world" and slogging through the mud. I expect many of us have had such experiences of intense beauty.

Participation in evolutionary religion allows one to contemplate the possibility—for given our skepticism, a possibility it is—that beauty is indeed at the heart of reality, just as in such moments it appears to be. If naturalism is true, this cannot be the case; however much and genuinely a naturalist may admire the beauty of nature, beauty is in an important sense only skin deep according to a naturalistic view of the world. And skepticism unmixed with anything else offers no response at all that might be worthy of such beauty. But by focusing on the idea of a nameless transcendence or ultimacy and imagining beauty to be (unavoidably for us) mysteriously deeper and indeed deepest in the nature of things, one can weave experiences of beauty more fully into life and pay a unique tribute, seeing the world as in some way it asks and *deserves* to be seen.

It is this notion of seeing things in nature as they deserve to be seen that I am trying to get at when I say that evolutionary religion can help us honor the world's intricate beauty. And it is the notion of "weaving experiences of beauty more fully into one's life" that I have in mind when I speak of doing justice to our most intense beauty-inspired experiences. Evolutionary religious faith allows us to give such experiences—experiences of a seemingly impenetrable and inexhaustible depth—an orienting significance in our lives appropriate to their power and persistence, instead of turning away under the influence of the thought that what they appear to reveal is only an appearance.

Some may label such an emphasis a runaway romanticism, finding more admirable a hardheaded realism that sees the world as cruel and ugly or as quite deeply mixed in its qualities. Perhaps in some temporal circumstances I would agree. But given how little, as hardheaded science attests, we may presently know of the world, if the love of beauty runs deep enough in us, we may come to respect the attitude that imagines it running deep in reality too.

Let's consider now the other pair of points—that evolutionary religion can help us to extend our appreciation of the world's beauty, and also to cultivate a concern for the preservation of the world's beauty and all that depends on it. We think of aesthetic appreciation as contributing to the highest and best ways of being human. But few of us act on this realization consistently. Although everyday events (even slogging through mud!) bring much aesthetic value to our mental door, much of it also stays outside: clearly we could discern and appreciate and integrate into our lives much more of the world's beauty if we paid more deliberate attention to it. And it is potentially one of the great virtues of evolutionary religion that it should constantly encourage us to do just this. In the practice of evolutionary religion, experiences of beauty will be regarded as possible intimations of a transcendent reality, and so we will be called to open ourselves more fully to all the detailed beauty of the natural world. Properly attempting to live by a religious proposition—especially a thin one, appropriate for beings still at an early pioneering stage aesthetically—means straining to find beauty wherever possible, and even where otherwise, deterred perhaps by some parochial preference, it might have been thought absent. Artists already possess the needed sensitivities and skills, and in the context of evolutionary religion they may be expected to assume a prophetic role.

Evolutionary faith could also assist us in *preserving and enhancing* the beautiful complexity of the world, including human life, in the face of all the environmental threats that could make our tenure on this planet brief indeed. Here we need to see that the dream of religion—if indeed the ultimate dream—can be of nothing less than a good embracing all that exists. If such fully inclusive religion were properly realized, its adherents would have to be in the vanguard of environmentalism broadly construed—as a movement of concern for all the world's ills; of a willingness to negotiate our place in nature with all who have a part in it, whether in the present or in the future; and of a determination correctly to identify and to resist all that we have made ugly instead of beautiful. And living within the framework provided by their faith ought to make it easier rather than more difficult for the imaginatively religious to persist with this vision and to navigate through all the obstacles that the future undoubtedly holds for our species. Because of the extra resources it would allow us to bring to these tasks, such faith should appear highly desirable.

Perhaps you'll be inclined to resist the alleged benefits of religious faith precisely at this point. You may be used to religion, through its complacency, making such things as environmental threats more serious instead of ameliorating them. Won't evolutionary religious faith be threatened by complacency too?

But the experience of temporal contextualization within which such faith arises forces us to contemplate a radical alteration in our self-conception. It requires us to imagine ourselves as limited and immature in many ways, as part of a process of development whose uncompleted portion may be ridiculously longer than that which our species has already gone through. It openly faces the possibility that we may not venture much further along that line into the future, that our existence may be no more than a wrinkle in the universe that time will finally smooth away. But it also allows us to imagine there being more to reality than the physical as currently construed: an unsurpassably good and beautiful "depth" or "center" in the nature of things toward which all things tend that we simply do not yet have the equipment to grasp with any security but that may dimly be glimpsed (as a chimp might dimly glimpse some of our realities) in certain elevated moments—perhaps even including experiences of beautifully intricate complexity.

And the faith I am defending grasps hold of this second imagining, though without losing the lesson of the first, and never settling into the security of confident belief. Thus in the balanced manner rightly associated with virtue, the attitude of evolutionary religion can avoid complacency while avoiding despair over our future, too, and persevering in the defense of all things beautiful.

This, at any rate, is what a skeptical but still wondering Paley might say in completion of his argument, after seeing the need to adapt religion to evolution.

JAMES'S WILL

I come now to the turn-of-the-twentieth-century American philosopher and psychologist William James, who, unlike Anselm, Leibniz, or Paley, is already associated by theists with the sort of "religious pragmatism" that my arguments in this chapter represent. James's famous essay defending what he calls "the will to believe" in matters of religion has been appealed to time and again by those who think that something more than or other than evidence ought to be involved in our judgments about religious belief. Their sort of reasoning often comes after Anselm, Leibniz, and Paley in the textbooks, and is called the *Pragmatic Argument for Belief in God*.

James once said that he should have changed the word "will" to "right" when formulating his essay's title. I'm inclined to think it's the word "believe" he should have changed. A diligent student of mine in an essay of his own once found in James's famous essay more than *twenty different ways* of referring to the attitude James is commending; and most of them seem to refer to something quite conscious, voluntary, and deliberate rather than to an involuntary "sense of reality." These variations are characteristic of James's work in philosophy, which, although containing systematic argument, is a glorious profusion of ideas, crisscrossing and overlapping in various ways. James is always seeing connections, and moves swiftly from one idea to others, subtly different but importantly connected. As a friend and colleague once put it to me: "James is often more concerned to associate than to disambiguate." Yes, indeed. And this can at times lead to unclarity and seeming inconsistency.

But three strands of Jamesian thought are worthy of recognition in our present context, and they come through quite clearly. Each can lend itself to the support of nonbelieving evolutionary religion even if, in part because of the intellectual dishonesty of trying on pragmatic grounds to get oneself out of a doubting attitude into a believing one, it is ineffective as a rational defense of theistic belief.

The Zestful Productivity Aim

First we have the idea that religion can bring us zest for living, and a framework within which such zest can continually be renewed. Religion can make us more energetic and productive people, and it simply makes life more interesting! In short, it's in our self-interest to be religious. If there is no distinct command from reason to *dis*believe, because of evident proofs of the falsehood of religion's claim about a reality greater than the natural and a universe that will ultimately prove to be on our side, then, says James, there is nothing wrong with following religion's lead when pursuing what I'll call the Zestful Productivity Aim.

Of course, in a situation of evolutionary skepticism, religious belief is, as we've seen, rationally ruled out. But this is when using "belief" in its normal sense, clarified (with James's help) in Chapter 3. If James has something else in mind here, something more like acceptance or assumption or acting-as-if or consenting imagination, then we're back to the races, rationally speaking, and the results of rational evaluation may well be different. And, of course, whatever James had in mind, we can *adapt* his reasoning to suit the purposes of evolutionary religion, especially if we think in terms of ultimism.

For the most interesting picture of the world, one might reasonably hold, is one in which the ultimate reality is as ultimism depicts it to be. Of course the crude crayon markings of much immature religion are disfiguring when added to the naturalist's sublimely simple depiction of reality. But we can aspire to more accomplished religious artistry. In particular, when focused simply on ultimism, evolutionary religion disfigures nothing, while adding to naturalism provocative ideas with greater depth and dimensionality, as well as a much greater positivity. And when through its positivity such religiousness brings zestful productivity, we have an added reason to be religious—and this even if we have fully absorbed evolutionary skepticism and set aside all detailed and believing forms of religiousness. Indeed, especially now, given the daunting challenges we primitives face in the struggle to carry our complex cultures into distant times, the Zestful Productivity Aim may commend itself to us, making evolutionary religion more desirable than it would otherwise be.

The Aim to Reconcile Competing Duties

The second strand of Jamesian reasoning I want to make use of is less straightforward. The aim it commends I will (somewhat cumbersomely) call the Aim to Reconcile Competing Duties. This argument builds on a central feature of "The Will to Believe": its distinction between our duty to avoid error, emphasized by those who urge an undiluted skepticism in a situation of evidential obscurity, and our duty to believe the truth. The discussion here is relevant to the one we entered into with Leibniz, as it concerns the aims of inquiry and the pursuit of understanding, but its point is made in a distinctive fashion. James says there are some truths—and he takes religious truths to be among them—that either *become* truths or are *seen to be* truths only when we take a risk and act accordingly even though the evidence is inconclusive. Thus those who wish to follow the duty to believe the truth should sometimes expect to fulfill this condition.

Take, for example (James has a similar example), the proposition that some new acquaintance is trustworthy. It may be only by assuming that this proposition is true and acting accordingly that you get evidence *proving* it is true. What if religious propositions were like that? Then by holding back, because of the impulse to avoid error, we would miss the truth—the most important truth of all. James concludes that we have a sort of intellectual stalemate here: no matter how one resolves the standoff between the two duties in the religious case, it can be argued that one has gone wrong. He therefore suggests that it is permissible to go with whatever passion is alive in one's heart—which for many people means "willing to believe."

Not much alteration is needed to turn this into another way of supporting evolutionary religion. Indeed, in our evolutionary context, with the bracing invitation to regard ourselves as early intellectual pioneers, James's point becomes more powerful. Here it may seem that according to the aims of the intellect alone (i.e. without reference to the passions) the religious choice is preferable—or reasonably regarded as such. In a situation as messy and undeveloped as ours, in which we have not yet taught any bell of absolute evidence to toll wherever truth exists, we must expect to be duped sometimes and to make risky choices in favor of a proposition if we want to be on the side of the most important truths, and to avoid living as though they are not truths. In our situation of immaturity, it would be even less surprising than it might otherwise be if the needed religious evidence were unavailable because obtaining it requires having faith that transcendence or ultimacy is realized and strenuously acting accordingly. At this early stage of the game, some lightness of heart and willingness to look beyond the available evidence must therefore be intellectually preferable to the heaviness and severe caution of those who order us to *wait* for stronger evidence—evidence that may just for that reason never come—before giving ourselves to imaginative faith.

And another point undergirds this one. Ironically, because of how an imaginative religious commitment with its underlay of evolutionary skepticism pushes us toward an even wider and deeper and more finegrained understanding of our experience and of the world than we might otherwise be motivated to take up, it can do justice not just to one side of the debate but to the other as well. If we think about it, we will see that by plunging ahead into a strenuously imaginative faith commitment, and living it out, we are, if anything, more likely to discover any facts counting *against* religious ideas there may be than if we hold back. Certainly, we cannot be put in a poorer position in this respect. And the one who holds back in skepticism or by accepting naturalism has nothing similar to say about facts potentially *supporting* religious claims. Thus an impartial consideration of our competing duties, it seems, must lead one toward evolutionary religion rather than away from it.

The Aim of Respect for What Ought To Be True

James's third strand of reasoning in support of religious commitment is as morally serious as his first argument was self-interestedly light. The human aim recommended here I call the Aim of Respect for What Ought To Be True. In James's final and unfinished work, published posthumously, this reasoning is presented—as it had been before, in other of his articles and books—in terms of something he calls a "faith-ladder":

1. There is nothing absurd in a certain view of the world being true, nothing self-contradictory.
2. It might have been true under certain conditions.
3. It may be true, even now.
4. It is fit to be true.
5. It ought to be true.
6. It must be true.
7. It shall be true, at any rate true for me.

What James's faith-ladder suggests is that there are propositions—and he includes religious propositions among them—that ought to be true even if they might not be true. At least part of what this means is that it would appropriately make us sad were these propositions to turn out to be false. Though James uses the word "faith," he seems here to be thinking of someone working herself into a state of belief in response to such propositions. But we need not take the steps of his ladder this way! We can think of imaginative faith instead. We can fasten on such faith as a "responsive gesture" which enables us to see possibilities of fulfillment and moral ideals as they *ought* to be seen if indeed they have the unrivaled importance our moral experience and commitment drive us to ascribe to them. (There is something analogous to a skeptical Paley's respect for beauty here.)

What is at issue is a powerful, teeth-gritting determination to imagine and live by what ought to be the case even if in fact it may not be the case—whenever the truth of what ought to be so is not ruled out by the evidence. Imagine a situation where (in circumstances of doubt) it ought to be the case that one finds one's way through a snowstorm on the Canadian prairie, or that one's child navigates safely through to the other side of depression or addictive behavior, or that the totalitarian party in power will be ousted, or that war can be made to cease. . . . Indeed, it is hard to imagine a case of the relevant sort in which faith is *not* called for, as a responsive gesture to the value one sees as sadly threatened. In all such cases, it appears that the best response—the response making the best whole of one's emotional and intellectual and other dispositions—will involve the attitudes of nonbelieving faith. So why would we deny that such faith is appropriate when we see how very much it ought to be the case that *ultimism* is true?

For it would be sad were the wonder of human conscious experience to cease just when individuals are starting to realize its benefits (or even before); and sad were the species—the whole project of human consciousness—to flicker out instead of flourishing ever more fully over the longest of runs. Consider especially the former matter, and let's put the point here more positively: ultimism, which tells us that the ultimate reality is ultimately valuable and the source of an ultimate good in which we can participate, leaves open the door to some sort of redemption for all those lives that have been and continually are being crushed, often before they have had a chance to be fully formed; and for this reason alone ultimism ought to be true. Taking up a life of imaginative faith, living as though ultimism *is* true, can therefore be something one does *for* those lives, as an appropriately serious moral gesture of respect or act of tribute. And it may itself attain respect-worthiness in circumstances like ours, where only religious skepticism, not outright religious disbelief, is justified by the available evidence.

Notice that this is not—certainly not—a gesture one makes as a substitute for the sort of active concern that might prevent lives from being crushed; nor should we expect unconcern about horrors gone through by those still living to be a corollary. It is all we can offer after the best such efforts have failed, and something we do while continuing to work on behalf of those still living.

Here the passions, so important to James, are obviously relevant. What do they say? That there is a Divine reality? No, hardly—but they can tell us that there ought to be! And, furthermore, they can tell us to follow this recognition into the responsive gesture of not just religious hope, which still timidly holds back, but the full imaginative commitment of religious faith.

* * *

Some will think, on a cursory glance at the idea of evolutionary religion, that it is quite beneath human dignity—undesirable and unworthy, a weak option liable to be rejected by anyone willing courageously to see the world as it is. But James's arguments, just like the other arguments we have formulated, show that one might sign on for such a commitment precisely *because* of how deeply one appreciates human dignity, both in oneself and in others. Furthermore, each of these arguments builds on an aim, whether aesthetic or intellectual or moral, that immature humans, pioneers in time, may reasonably take up precisely in order to become stronger and more mature—the Enlargement Aim, the Aim of Understanding, the Aim of Respect for Beauty, the Zestful Productivity Aim, the Aim to Reconcile Competing Duties, and the Aim of Respect for What

Ought to Be True. Together these aims span the whole of life as we know it. If we agree that the pursuit of such aims is admirable or desirable, given our temporal condition, and that evolutionary religion provides the best way of pursuing them (especially where they are conjoined), then we will agree, furthermore, that evolutionary religion is fully appropriate to our place in time. Moreover, we will conclude that those historically famous theistic arguments associated with Anselm, Leibniz, Paley, and James, even if quite unsuccessful as attempts to justify theistic belief, can indeed be adapted to support evolutionary faith, just as the hypothesis we set out to test would have it.

For what the adapted arguments show is that through imaginative evolutionary faith we are best able to *express* and *honor* and also *further develop and support into the future* the beautiful but fragile, multi-faceted and value-laden complexity that can be seen in the process of becoming human, as realized at various levels in individuals, communities, and the species at large. Notice especially the last part of this summary. Evolutionary religion, if designed to fit us and our time, will toughen us for a loving assault on the next 10,000 years. It looks not for consolation and an escape from the world as it is but for a pioneering hope and determination that may be spent on behalf of others and a world still being born.

Epilogue: Darwin's Door and Hegel's Hinge

Evolutionary biologists sometimes speak of the hominin line that was able to take on the bulky Neanderthals and spread across Europe some 50,000 years ago as more "gracile"—slender, light-boned, nimble—than both their antecedents and their adversaries. Gracility brought versatility, and proved to be an advantage. In this book I hope to have shown that by approaching matters of religion with genuine curiosity, pursuing conceptual clarity, scientific implications, and humanistic concern far enough and in combination (averse to overhasty or onesided conclusions, like Darwin himself), we may yet find a way for religion to evolve into a more gracile imaginative-skeptical form of life appropriate to our time.

Evolutionists, as we've seen, have told us at most half the story about religion. To do better, we need to survey the *whole* of Earthly time, finding our place in it. What we will then discover is an exciting new way of making sense of religion that all parts of the culture can appreciate. Our understanding of faith naturally must experience something of a "downsizing" to make it fit the primitives we are, but there is abundant reason already to suppose that in the new dispensation, given temporal contextualization, faith will for the first time be in a position to win an unequivocal endorsement from all who wish to deepen humanity's acquaintance with truth, beauty, and goodness.

What could make our culture *actually* evolve in some such fashion, stepping boldly into the new territory Darwin's Door has opened up to us? The nineteenth-century German thinker Georg Wilhelm Friedrich Hegel was the sort of philosopher—Kant was another—whose works Darwin would dip into now and then while professing to profit little from the encounter. But even Darwin had probably heard attributed to Hegel this famous idea: that the opposition between one intellectual option (thesis) and another (antithesis) can often be

resolved at a higher level of truth (synthesis). Now, there is controversy among scholars as to whether Hegel really affirmed this idea,
and, if so, just what he meant by it. But set all that aside. This idea, so
I want to suggest in closing, can be put to work here, as a way of
motivating us to actually take the steps proposed in this book. It
provides the appropriate sort of *hinge* for Darwin's Door.

For many millennia religious belief, sanctioned by both inner and
outer authority, had the world stage to itself. From the rituals of
hunter-gatherers and early social groups to the more sophisticated
religious institutions of city states and finally of world religions like
Christianity, a view of reality confidently supernaturalistic long held
sway. Let this traditionally religious confidence be our Hegelian *thesis*.

But in recent centuries, and especially in the west, as a result of
complex social and intellectual conditions first arising in the eight-
eenth century, collectively known as "the Enlightenment," the cultural power of religion has been on the wane and naturalistic thinking
has been on the rise. The Enlightenment stands for "progressive" and
"liberal" and above all for "rational" thinking. And "rational" has
tended to bump hard into "religious"—never more so than since the
advent of Darwinian evolution. Enlightenment thought, regarded as
embracing the various impulses I have mentioned and fueled by
evolution, provides our Hegelian *antithesis*.

These two, thesis and antithesis, have for some time now been
battling it out, and the prevailing assumption appears to be that one
or the other must give in, or else the two must learn how to operate in
completely separate domains, having tucked neatly out of the way the
unruly bits—such as the idea of a transcendent reality—that provoke
conflict. *But if evolutionary religion is really possible, then a whole new
option opens up.* Then there is a way of taking the best from Enlightenment thought and religion, as currently conceived, including the
offending idea of an ultimate transcendent reality, and producing
something new "at a higher level of truth."

If Darwin's Door opens smoothly for our culture and stays open,
instead of silently closing as once again we look to the past, it will be
because we recognize the momentousness of this possibility. The
momentousness consists in no less than this: that with the idea of
evolutionary religion we are led from the thesis of traditional religious
belief and the antithesis of Enlightenment thought to a new synthesis
of ideas both religious and rational well fitted to stimulate and guide
the next stages of human evolution.

NOTES

PROLOGUE

p. 1: **A detective novel written by a good philosopher.** . . . The joke originates in "Literary Boredom," by Jonathan Wolff (who is also a philosopher), *The Guardian*, Tuesday, September 4, 2007.

p. 2: **"the infancy of our species"** Christopher Hitchens, *God is not Great: How Religion Poisons Everything* (New York: Twelve Books, 2007), p. 64.

p. 3: **"an abstract, intellectual understanding of deep time comes easily enough. . . . "** Stephen Jay Gould, *Time's Arrow, Time's Cycle* (Cambridge, MA: Harvard University Press, 1987), p. 3.

p. 3: **The average lifespan.** . . . Here I have been helped by Robert M. May, "Conceptual aspects of the quantification of the extent of biological diversity," in D. L. Hawksworth, ed., *Biodiversity: Measurement and Estimation* (Oxford: The Royal Society, 2005).

p. 4: **. . . we are still in the beginning.** Whether talk of our species being at a beginning or at "an early stage" is appropriate depends on whether age or extent of development is being made a function of (i) how long our species will actually endure or how far it will actually advance in one respect or another; (ii) how long species of our kind typically endure or how far they typically advance; or (iii) how long it is possible for our species or species like ours to endure or how far we may possibly advance, with possibility here meaning *epistemic* possibility (see Chapter 3 for more on that). A similar point applies to more general talk of *intelligence* being at a beginning point or at an early stage of development. Now, (i) can be ruled out as a standard here for the same reason making it ridiculous to think of a child aged one month who is destined to die tomorrow as old or fully developed. (An exception arises when one uses expressions confining oneself to the actual life of our species, as when one says that we are at an early stage "in human history." This clearly may not be the case! And that is why I avoid all such confining expressions when I say that we *are* at a beginning instead of only that we *may* be.) (ii) seems better because the child would properly be said to be at the beginning of life or at an early stage of development as judged by how long humans (beings of its kind) typically endure or how far they typically develop. I was implicitly appealing to this standard a page or so ago in the text. But (ii) won't always help us. For example, if species of the relevant kind are ones engaged in systematic inquiry, then there *aren't* any (other than ourselves). In such a case we need to move on to (iii), which is what I often do in the book.

p. 4: ... an intriguing question about evolution and religion ... When speaking about religion in this book, and certainly when promoting it, I will generally have in mind religion as practice or way of life, whether individual or communal; *religiousness* rather than any complex institutional entity straddling the centuries of the sort we call "a religion." In my *Prolegomena to a Philosophy of Religion* (Ithaca: Cornell University Press, 2005) I call this the *personal* sense of the term "religion."

p. 6: I have developed similar views before in three books ... The books are *Prolegomena to a Philosophy of Religion*, *The Wisdom to Doubt: A Justification of Religious Skepticism*, and *The Will to Imagine: A Justification of Skeptical Religion*, published by Cornell University Press in 2005, 2007, and 2009, respectively.

CHAPTER 1

p. 8: "Our brains are built to deal with events on radically different timescales. ..." Richard Dawkins, *The Blind Watchmaker* (London: Penguin Books, 2006), p. xix.

p. 10: ... James Hutton showed his friend John Playfair an "unconformity" ... The story of Hutton and Playfair appears in many places. My version is based largely on the account of Gould in *Time's Arrow, Time's Cycle*.

p. 10: "The impression made will not easily be forgotten" ... John Playfair, "Biographical account of the late Dr. James Hutton, F. R. S.," *Transactions of the Royal Society of Edinburgh* 5 (Part 3) (1802): 73.

p. 11: ... Playfair's beautifully written restatement ... See John Playfair, *Illustrations of the Huttonian Theory of the Earth* (Cambridge: Cambridge University Press, 2011).

p. 11: "Principles of Geology" ... The ninth edition may be accessed free of charge at Project Gutenberg: <http://www.gutenberg.org/ebooks/33224> last accessed November 23, 2012.

p. 12: ... 24 million years old, in his last pronouncement. ... Bill Bryson, *A Short History of Nearly Everything* (Toronto: Anchor Canada, 2003), p. 78.

p. 12: Darwin's writings show that he experienced considerable anxiety. ... Janet Browne, *Charles Darwin: The Power of Place* (Princeton: Princeton University Press, 2002), p. 315.

p. 13: "If the history of the Earth were represented by the old English measure of a yard. ..." John McPhee, *Basin and Range* (New York: Farrar, Straus, and Giroux, 1980), p. 126.

p. 13: "An understanding of the process of stellar evolution. ..." Richard W. Pogge, "The once and future sun": <http://www.astronomy.ohio-state.edu/~pogge/Lectures/vistas97.html> last accessed October 29, 2012.

p. 13: . . . developed in the 1980s by Douglas Gough. . . . See D. O. Gough, "Solar interior structure and luminosity variations," *Solar Physics* (1981): 21–34.

p. 14: " . . . the present Sun is increasing its average luminosity. . . ." K. P. Schroeder and Robert Connon Smith, "Distant future of the Sun and Earth revisited," *Monthly Notices of the Royal Astronomical Society* 386 (2008): 157.

p. 14: As the Caltech press release explained. . . . <http://media.caltech.edu/press_releases/13266> last accessed October 29, 2012.

p. 15: . . . when our brain cells first really started clicking some 50,000 years ago. . . . The 50,000 year figure is based on Richard Klein's influential *The Human Career*, 2nd edn (Chicago: University of Chicago Press, 1999). Some scientists would say that the relevant figure is more like 100,000 years. It will not matter for my argument which way we go on this; readers may mentally adjust the figure as they deem appropriate.

p. 17: "fifty-fifty" Martin Rees, *Our Final Century* (London: Arrow Books, 2003), p. 8.

p. 19: "If you come across a garter snake. . . . " Nicholas Kristof, "When Our Brains Short-Circuit," *New York Times*, July 1, 2009.

CHAPTER 2

p. 22: "We may be certain that the ordinary succession by generation has never once been broken. . . . " Charles Darwin, *The Origin of Species* (London: Penguin Books, 1985 [1859]), p. 459.

p. 22: "too profound . . . " See Janet Browne, *Charles Darwin: The Power of Place* (Princeton: Princeton University Press, 2002), p. 176.

p. 23: "If the tree of life goes on growing. . . . " Christian de Duve, "Constraints on the origin and evolution of life," in *The Challenges of Sciences: A Tribute to the Memory of Carlos Chagas* (The Vatican: The Pontifical Institute of Sciences, 2002), pp. 110–11.

p. 24: "That's stupid!": <http://www.vega.org.uk/video/programme/126> last accessed November 5, 2012.

p. 25: "What was extraordinary about human development. . . . " Ronald Wright, *A Short History of Progress* (Toronto: Anansi Press, 2004), p. 13.

p. 25: "we can fly above the tallest mountains. . . . " Jerry A. Coyne, *Why Evolution is True* (New York: Penguin, 2009), p. 233.

p. 26: . . . important social technologies . . . Perhaps development toward greater social and emotional sophistication will be aided by natural selection. For example, some biologists see a trend in biological evolution toward an ever greater capacity for others-oriented caring. See Jeffrey P. Schloss, "Would Venus evolve on Mars? Bioenergetic constraints, allometric trends, and the evolution of life-history invariants," in J. D. Barrow et al., eds. *Fitness of the Cosmos for Life: Biochemistry and Fine-Tuning* (Cambridge: Cambridge University Press, 2007), pp. 318–46.

p. 26: "This represents only one-thousandth of the total time. . . ." Coyne, *Why Evolution is True*, p. 227.

p. 27: "domed cities, linear cities, underground cities. . . ." Doug Cocks, *Deep Futures: Our Prospects for Survival* (Montreal: McGill-Queen's University Press, 2003), p. 86.

p. 27: Perhaps it was the favoring, by natural selection. . . . See Nicholas Wade, *Before the Dawn: Recovering the Lost History of Our Ancestors* (New York: Penguin, 2006), pp. 98–9.

p. 27: This is suggested by the respected molecular geneticist Roy Britten. . . . See Roy Britten, "Transposable element insertions have strongly affected human evolution," *Proceedings of the National Academy of Science* 107 (2010): 19945–8.

p. 28: "perhaps our distant descendants will be far more intelligent. . . ." Wade, *Before the Dawn*, pp. 275, 276.

p. 28: "the speed of information processing. . . ." Steven Pinker, *The Better Angels of Our Nature: Why Violence Has Declined* (New York: Viking, 2011), p. 653.

p. 28: "upper limit" . . . An audio version of Conway Morris's 2000 Gifford Lectures is available at <http://www.iscast.org/conway_morris_bio> last accessed November 5, 2012. The comments about the brain appear in Lecture Four.

p. 29: . . . with Wade and his sources. . . . See Wade, *Before the Dawn*, p. 71.

p. 29: "mere juveniles" See the abstract for Lecture Four of Simon Conway Morris's Gifford Lectures, at: <http://www.hss.ed.ac.uk/giffordexemp/2000/details/ProfessorSimonConwayMorris.html>, last accessed November 5, 2012.

p. 30: "declines of biomes and biotas" . . . David S. Woodruff, "Declines of Biomes and Biotas and the Future of Evolution": <http://www.pnas.org/content/98/10/5471.full> last accessed November 5, 2012.

p. 31: "new great and wondrous beasts will inevitably evolve. . . ." Robert M. Hazen, *The Story of Earth* (New York: Viking, 2012), p. 282.

p. 32: . . . contributors to a fascinating recent book. . . . See Damien Broderick, ed., *Year Million: Science at the Far Edge of Knowledge* (New York: Atlas & Co., 2008).

p. 32: . . . as the guru of transhumanism, Ray Kurzweil would have it. . . . See Ray Kurzweil, *The Singularity is Near: When Humans Transcend Biology* (New York: Viking, 2005).

CHAPTER 3

p. 34: "There are many questions. . . . " Bertrand Russell, *The Problems of Philosophy* (Oxford: Oxford University Press, 1919), p. 155.

p. 34: "[Humans] plainly have the capacity to solve certain problems. . . . " Noam Chomsky, *Language and the Problems of Knowledge* (Cambridge, MA: MIT Press, 1988), p. 149.

p. 34: "a clashing of analytically honed intellects. . . . " Colin McGinn, *The Making of a Philosopher* (New York: HarperCollins), p. 63.

p. 35: "combinatorial atomism with lawlike mappings. . . . " Colin McGinn, *Problems in Philosophy: The Limits of Inquiry* (Oxford: Blackwell, 1993), pp. 18, 30, 150.

p. 35: I suggest we assume that McGinn is on to something. . . . Alvin Plantinga, long at Notre Dame University, has recently argued that we face an even more thoroughgoing evolutionary challenge than the one implicit in McGinn, one applicable to *all* our beliefs—at least if we assume, as perhaps most evolutionists do, that natural selection is not in any way guided by an intelligence (or Intelligence). This, says Plantinga, is because we have no good reason to suppose that the truth of our beliefs would *matter* at all to unguided natural selection. On his view, all that matters in a system governed by natural selection is that the beliefs we hold, whatever they are, get us behaving in survival-conducive ways. Thus if we assume that evolutionary theory is correct and natural selection unguided, we have no good reason to regard our cognitive faculties as reliable. (For Plantinga's argument and numerous replies, see James K. Beilby, ed. *Naturalism Defeated? Essays on Plantinga's Evolutionary Argument Against Naturalism* (Ithaca: Cornell University Press, 2002).) In producing his challenge, Plantinga is taking a page from a certain sort of skepticism, known as global skepticism, which I'll be discussing shortly. Or maybe we should say he's adding a page, since he has offered global skepticism another reason to cite in skeptical reasoning: an evolutionary one. In any case, I hold that the same reply I will be offering the global skeptic can be used by any evolutionist in a reply to Plantinga. For this reason I don't set his past-oriented evolutionary argument alongside McGinn's.

p. 36: . . . which casts many of our treasured beliefs into question. . . . If you think belief need not be unjustified even in the absence of the truth-oriented reasons for believing philosophers care about, then a discussion of the nature of belief coming up soon may be helpful: belief is involuntary and by its very nature connected to truth, so it would take self-deception—something non-philosophers too can see to be a problem—to try to believe without truth-oriented reasons.

p. 38: "hinges" . . . Ludwig Wittgenstein, *On Certainty* (Oxford: Basil Blackwell, 1969), # 341.

p. 38: **All things considered, then, we are quite reasonable.** ... I'll often be defining my terms. But not all terms—even all important terms—can or will be defined. Sometimes I will just assume that our inhabiting a common linguistic universe makes it the case that whatever you understand by the term in question will be close enough to suit my purposes. That is how it will be with the terms "reasonable" and "unreasonable" and also certain related expressions such as "ought not be held." (Another reason for not discriminating between competing interpretations here is that they themselves may be subject to skepticism.)

p. 39: ... **it may often seem a matter of indifference whether it is believed.** To some this may suggest a "postmodern" approach, but the thing to remember is that here the expectation of old fashioned knowledge and cognitive contact with reality is only *postponed*, in view of our place at the beginning of intelligent inquiry, not given up altogether, as so often in postmodern perspectives on knowledge.

p. 40: **"the sense of reality"** William James, *The Principles of Psychology*, vol. 2 (Cambridge, MA: Harvard University Press, 1981), p. 913.

p. 41: **"there were at least two contemporary Homo species. ... "** John Noble Wilford, "New fossils indicate early branching of human family tree," *New York Times*, August 8, 2012.

p. 43: **In philosophy of science there is the famous "pessimistic induction".** ... For a good survey of argumentation concerning the pessimistic induction, see P. Kyle Stanford, *Exceeding Our Grasp: Science, History, and the Problem of Unconceived Alternatives* (Oxford: Oxford University Press, 2006). Stanford himself comes close, in some of what he says, to the sort of skepticism developed here, but he is still focused on the *history* of science and on what might be available in our evidence but unconceived right now.

p. 45: **Suppose you have no familiarity with the game of basketball.** ... I owe this example to Paul Draper. He was going to use it to explain my views in a review of my book *The Wisdom to Doubt* but in the end didn't have room to include it. He kindly agreed for me to use it here instead.

p. 51: **In contemporary epistemology, this issue of peer disagreement looms large.** ... See, for example, Richard Feldman and Ted A. Warfield, eds. *Disagreement* (Oxford: Oxford University Press, 2010).

p. 53: **McGinn doesn't have much time for the idea that the future could change things.** McGinn, *Problems in Philosophy*, p. 152.

CHAPTER 4

p. 55: **"My mind is not closed. ... "** *Time*, November 5, 2006.

p. 59: **"What I see in Nature is a magnificent structure. ... "** Quoted in Richard Dawkins, *The God Delusion* (New York: Houghton Mifflin, 2006), p. 15.

p. 59: **In Einstein's stretched sense of the word, Dawkins has said, he is religious, too.** Dawkins, *God Delusion*, p. 19.

p. 59: **"pretty childish"** Dennis Overbye, "Einstein letter on God sells for $404,000," *New York Times*, May 17, 2008.

p. 61: **"asymptotic decrease. ... "** ... Barbara Forrest, "Methodological naturalism and philosophical naturalism: clarifying the connection," *Philo* 3 (2000), 25.

p. 68: **"spiritual genius"** Karen Armstrong, *The Great Transformation* (Toronto: Random House, 2007), p. 474.

p. 69: **"are best adapted to the narrow limits of human understanding"** David Hume, *Enquiry concerning Human Understanding*, in *Enquiries concerning Human Understanding and concerning the Principles of Morals*, edited by L. A. Selby-Bigge, 3rd edn revised by P. H. Nidditch (Oxford: Clarendon Press, 1975), p. 162.

CHAPTER 5

p. 71: **In the statement that accompanies his portrait. ...** The portrait and statement may be accessed at: <http://www.pyke-eye.com/view/phil_II_25.html> last accessed November 23, 2012.

p. 71: **"higher aesthetic tastes"** ... Nora Barlow, ed., *The Autobiography of Charles Darwin, 1809–1882, with Original Omissions Restored* (London: Collins, 1958), p. 139.

p. 80: ... **the Oxford philosopher Richard Swinburne. ...** See his *Faith and Reason*, 2nd edn (Oxford: Clarendon Press, 2005).

p. 80: **The latter idea of beliefless trust is developed and defended by Robert Audi. ...** "Belief, faith, and acceptance," *International Journal for Philosophy of Religion* 63 (2008): 87–102.

p. 80: ... **the former of beliefless assumption by philosopher Daniel Howard-Snyder of Western Washington University.** "Schellenberg on propositional faith," *Religious Studies*, 48 (2013) forthcoming.

p. 80: **"To accept that p. ... "** L. Jonathan Cohen, *An Essay on Belief and Acceptance* (Oxford: Clarendon Press, 1992), p. 4.

p. 81: **Thus we have William Alston. ...** See William P. Alston, "Belief, acceptance, and religious faith," in Jeff Jordan and Daniel Howard-Snyder, eds., *Faith, Freedom, and Rationality* (Lanham, MD: Rowman & Littlefield, 1996).

p. 82: **"needs to undergo a second transformation. ... "** ... Nicholas Wade, *The Faith Instinct: How Religion Evolved and Why it Endures* (New York: Penguin, 2009), p. 285.

p. 82: "I also hope, and expect. . . . ": <http://firedoglake.com/2009/06/
28/fdl-book-salon-welcomes-robert-wright-the-evolution-of-god/> last
accessed November 23, 2012.

p. 82: "there's room" . . . Robert Wright, *The Evolution of God* (New York:
Little, Brown and Company, 2009), pp. 427, 442, 483.

p. 85: . . . Christian de Duve's latest book. . . . See Christian de Duve,
*Genetics of Original Sin: The Impact of Natural Selection on the Future of
Humanity* (New Haven: Yale University Press, 2012).

p. 85: E. O. Wilson has made a similar point. . . . See Edward O. Wilson, *The
Creation: An Appeal to Save Life on Earth* (New York: W. W. Norton,
2006).

p. 86: They are exemplified by Gretta Vospers. . . . See Gretta Vospers, *With
or Without God* (New York: HarperCollins, 2008).

CHAPTER 6

p. 91: "The principles which ought to govern. . . . " John Stuart Mill, *Three
Essays on Religion*, 4th edn (London: Longmans, Green, Reader, and Dyer,
1875), pp. 244–5.

p. 92: "never had it" John Stuart Mill, *Autobiography* (London: Longmans,
Green, Reader, and Dyer, 1873), p. 43.

p. 92: "To me it seems that human life, small and confined as it is. . . . " Mill,
Three Essays, p. 245.

p. 94: A Divine reality is supposed to be "more" in all three of these
ways. . . . The question of the nature of religion is notoriously contentious.
I have addressed it at greater length in Chapter 1 of my *Prolegomena to a
Philosophy of Religion* (Ithaca: Cornell University Press, 2005), but questions may remain. If you disagree with me, and especially if you disagree
with me on historical grounds, perhaps because of facts about ancient
Greek religion or some such thing, then you may take me to be drawing
out ideas common to a *very wide stretch* of religion, including the forms of
religion most influential today, and proposing that we seek in some
fashion to preserve them into the future.

p. 96: . . . the Divine is *not* in all three spheres ultimate. This proposition
does not imply that the Divine is *non*-ultimate in *all three* spheres. It is
compatible with ultimacy in, say, two out of the three. And what this
shows is that there are other options between Weak and Strong. (Some of
these are treated by Jeanine Diller in "The conceptual focus of ultimism: an
object of religious concern for the nones and somes," *Religious Studies*, 48
(2013) forthcoming.) I am ignoring them here both because I have already
tried the reader's patience with my distinctions and because a fuller
discussion would not affect the outcomes of this section's discussion.

p. 96: Others, such as his American contemporary William James.... See Lecture XX of James's *The Varieties of Religious Experience* (New York: Penguin Books, 1982 [1902]).

p. 96:...and the more recent Harvard philosopher Robert Nozick.... Robert Nozick, *The Examined Life: Philosophical Meditations* (New York: Simon & Shuster, 1989), chap. 5.

p. 96: And there are philosophers writing today who think this is or may be the right way to go. See, for example, Diller, "The conceptual focus of ultimism" and Thomas M. Crisp, "On coercion, love, and horrors," *Religious Studies*, 48 (2013) forthcoming.

p. 97: ...as thinkers such as Feuerbach and Freud and also the recently developed cognitive science of religion suggest.... See Ludwig Feuerbach, *The Essence of Religion* (Amherst: Prometheus Books, 2004) and Sigmund Freud, *The Future of an Illusion* (New York: W. W. Norton, 1990). On cognitive science of religion, see Todd Tremlin, *Minds and Gods: The Cognitive Foundations of Religion* (Oxford: Oxford University Press, 2006).

p. 99: "one god, greatest among gods and men...."... Quoted in Norman Melchert, *The Great Conversation*, vol. 1: *Pre-Socratics Through Descartes*, 4th ed. (New York: McGraw-Hill, 2002), p. 16; see also p. 15.

p. 102: "a distinct cognitive attitude (DCA)" The term was originated by Timothy Schroeder and Carl Matheson. See their "Imagination and Emotion," in *The Architecture of the Imagination: New Essays on Pretense, Possibility, and Fiction*, ed. Shaun Nichols, (Oxford: Clarendon Press, 2006), p. 19.

p. 102: "imaginings are distinguished from beliefs by their pattern of causal interaction"... Shaun Nichols, "Introduction," in *The Architecture of the Imagination*, p. 8.

p. 102: "sending impulses to emotional centers like the orbitofrontal cortex...." Schroeder and Matheson, "Imagination and Emotion," p. 28.

p. 102:...Nichols reminds us that even hungry children.... "Introduction," p. 7.

p. 104: Yet when, in later life, Darwin responded to letters about *religious* faith.... Janet Browne, *Charles Darwin: The Power of Place* (Princeton: Princeton University Press, 2002), p. 391.

p. 110: ...somewhat like people sent out by the Mennonite Central Committee.... See: <http://mcccanada.ca/> last accessed November 15, 2012.

p. 114: "neoagnostic" Winifred Gallagher, *Working on God* (New York: Random House, 1999), p. xiv.

p. 115: "Imaging a wider *we* does not mean leaving our separate communities behind...." Diana L. Eck, *Encountering God: A Spiritual Journey from Bozeman to Banaras* (Boston: Beacon Press, 2003), pp. 227–8.

CHAPTER 7

p. 116: "Such is the sum of the several chief objections...." Charles Darwin, *Origin of Species* (London: Penguin Books, 1985 [1859]), p. 440.

p. 116: "The word *philosophy* means...." Robert Nozick, *The Nature of Rationality* (Princeton: Princeton University Press, 1993), p. xi.

p. 116: "one long argument" Darwin, *Origin of Species*, p. 435.

p. 123: "permanent experiential blank" Wes Morriston, "Is faith in the ultimate rationally required? Taking issue with some arguments in *The Will to Imagine*," *Religious Studies*, 48 (2013) forthcoming.

p. 131: "the rectitude of the intellect...."... John Stuart Mill, *Three Essays on Religion*, 4th edn (London: Longmans, Green, Reader, and Dyer, 1875), pp. 244–9.

p. 132: "The fuzziness of these New-Age sounding attitudes...." Jeffrey Jordan, "On joining the ranks of the faithful": <http://www.infidels.org/library/modern/jeffrey_jordan/faith.html> accessed November 15, 2012.

p. 133: As the cognitive science of religion (CSR) is starting to reveal.... See Justin Barrett, *Why Would Anyone Believe in God?* (Lanham, MD: AltaMira Press, 2004).

p. 136: "the Nones increased from 8.1 percent...": <http://commons.trincoll.edu/aris/files/2011/08/NONES_08.pdf> accessed November 15, 2012.

CHAPTER 8

p. 137: "We are just at the beginning of a new age of religious searching. ..." Charles Taylor, *A Secular Age* (Cambridge, MA: Harvard University Press, 2007), p. 535.

p. 138: I have some arguments that just may do the job. For a more detailed treatment of them, see my book *The Will to Imagine: A Justification of Skeptical Religion* (Ithaca: Cornell University Press, 2009).

p. 140: ...Anselm claims that he can prove from this idea alone.... See Proslogion 2 in *Anselm of Canterbury: The Major Works*, ed. Brian Davies and G. R. Evans (Oxford: Oxford University Press, 1998).

p. 140: Even the great mathematician Kurt Gödel thought he might have a way of making the argument work. See Graham Oppy, *Ontological Arguments and Belief in God* (Cambridge: Cambridge University Press, 1995), pp. 224–5.

p. 143: ...nowhere is his ambition more evident or deeper.... See Gottfried Wilhelm Leibniz, *Principles of Nature and Grace, Based on Reason*, 7, in *G. W. Leibniz: Philosophical Texts*, trans. Richard Francks and R. S. Woolhouse (Oxford: Oxford University Press, 1998).

p. 146: **Paley's argument for Divine design.** . . . See William Paley, *Natural Theology* (Oxford: Oxford University Press, 2008).

p. 146: **Richard Dawkins has expressed a kind of affection for Paley.** . . . See Richard Dawkins, *The Blind Watchmaker* (London: Penguin Books, 2006), p. 4.

p. 150: **"the will to believe"** See William James, *The Will to Believe, Human Immortality, and Other Essays in Popular Philosophy* (New York: Dover, 1956).

p. 153: **"faith-ladder"** . . . William James, *Some Problems of Philosophy* (Cambridge, MA: Harvard University Press, 1979), p. 113.

Index